"LET US MAKE MAN . . ."

LET US make man

PASTOR
JAMES LEE BEALL

WHITAKER BOOKS

1972

WHITAKER BOOKS
504 Laurel Drive
Monroeville, Pennsylvania 15146

PRINTED IN THE UNITED STATES OF AMERICA

DEDICATION

*To my good wife, Anne. Her love and deep strength
have made a difference.*

FOREWORD

Jesus said to His disciples, "Behold, I send you out as lambs in the midst of wolves" (Luke 10:3). Of all the helpless pictures this is the most helpless and most hopeless: "lambs in the midst of wolves." They haven't a ghost of a chance to survive, for they were not even full-grown sheep. A sheep, full-grown, at least had a chance of running away from the wolves, but lambs can't fight or run. Lambs are a symbol of complete helplessness. Yet when the Book of Revelation closes, it depicts THE LAMB upon the throne. The lamb had conquered the wolves! The Lamb was on the throne, the ruler. How did it happen?

It wasn't by chance. It was the manifestation of a superior force, the power of love.

In this book it has been my purpose to explore the working of God in all avenues of life and living and to show nothing has ever gotten out-of-hand with God—He is in full charge of everything.

It seems to me that most Christians have been made overly aware of Satan and what he can do. Some seem to propose that every negative thought in the human mind has been placed there by Satan. Others have given to Satan the same attributes only possessed by the Lord God. We need a housecleaning of the mind in these areas.

The messages that appear in this book were taken from

weekly radio scripts and edited into their present form. They were enthusiastically received all over the country.

It is my sincere hope that when you finish reading this book your eyes will behold the goodness, the beauty, and the power of God in a new and wonderful way.

Pastor James L. Beall

CONTENTS

	FOREWORD	7
1.	SUFFERING AND GLORY	11
2.	TOUCHING THE GLORY	21
3.	LUCIFER AND AUTHORITY	31
4.	LUCIFER'S CRASH	41
5.	ORDER OUT OF CHAOS	49
6.	THE STRUGGLE FOR DOMINION	59
7.	THE DECLARATION OF WAR	67
8.	THE ORGANIZATION OF ANGELS	77
9.	THE COURT OF HEAVEN	87
10.	KNOWING OUR ENEMY	97
11.	RUNNING BEFORE OUR TIME	105
12.	CAPTIVATED MINDS	113
13.	ATTACKS AGAINST THE SOUL	121
14.	THE ORIGIN OF DEMONS	129
15.	UNDERSTANDING DEMON POSSESSION	141
16.	WHAT IS DEMON POSSESSION	151
17.	CAN A BELIEVER BE DEMON POSSESSED?	161
18.	SONS BY ADOPTION	171
19.	CHILDREN OF GOD	179
20.	HEIRS AND JOINT HEIRS	187
21.	SUFFERING AND GLORY	197

CHAPTER ONE

SUFFERING AND GLORY

"The manifestation of the sons of God" is a very strange phrase which is taken from the words of the Apostle Paul to the Romans, a phrase which has been the subject of many sermons and writings.

"For I reckon that the sufferings of this present time are not worthy to be compared with the glory which shall be revealed in us.

"For the earnest expectation of the creature waiteth for the manifestation of the sons of God.

"For the creature was made subject to vanity, not willingly, but by reason of him who hath subjected the same in hope.

"Because the creature itself also shall be delivered from the bondage of corruption into the glorious liberty of the children of God.

"For we know that the whole creation groaneth and travaileth in pain together until now.

"And not only they, but ourselves also, which have the first-fruit of the Spirit, even we ourselves groan

within ourselves, waiting for the adoption, to wit,
the redemption of our body."

(Romans 8:18–23)

In these verses Paul talks about the thought which is our
subject, "the manifestation of the sons of God." What can
this possibly mean? Evidently it means very much to Paul to
cause him to write these words. He must have seen something tremendously glorious and wonderful.

In this first chapter I want to deal in particular with the
eighteenth verse.

"For I reckon that the sufferings of this present
time are not worthy to be compared with the glory
which shall be revealed in us."

When a man speaks like this, you can be sure he has seen
something to make such a definite comparison. It was as
though Paul had arranged his joys and sorrows into two
columns to make a comparison. On the one side he listed his
sufferings; on the other side, the glories he knew were to
come. The Apostle Paul did some reckoning here and he
came up with a definite answer. This word "reckon" is
"logizomai" in the Greek language. This means literally: a
mathematical calculation, a shrewd observation, a proper
deduction, a thoughtful estimate, a studied conclusion, and a
careful reckoning.

Paul put all his experiences together and began to differ-
entiate between them like a bookkeeper does with his credits
and debits. Paul took into account all the happenings of his
life and weighed each one carefully. He prepared a spiritual
ledger and from it he drew a balance sheet with an enormous
credit balance. On the one side of his spiritual ledger he

12

placed all the debits—his sufferings. On the other side, he listed the credits—the glories he had seen. Then he totaled the two columns and reached a studied conclusion. His answer revealed whether or not it was worthwhile to follow Christ and be His apostle.

Paul listed the debits in 2 Cor. 11:23–28:

"...in stripes above measure, in prisons more frequent, in deaths oft.

"Of the Jews five times received I forty stripes save one.

"Thrice was I beaten with rods, once was I stoned, thrice I suffered shipwreck, a night and a day I have been in the deep;

"In journeyings often, in perils of waters, in perils of robbers, in perils by mine own countrymen, in perils by the heathen, in perils in the city, in perils in the wilderness, in perils in the sea, in perils among false brethren;

"In weariness and painfulness, in watchings often, in hunger and thirst, in fastings often, in cold and nakedness.

"Besides those things that are without, that which comes upon me daily, the care of all the churches."

This is the list of Paul's debits—everything that had gone against him. All his problems and sufferings were very real but Paul did not have a persecution complex. Why? He knew he had suffered for a reason. He could trace his sufferings and misunderstandings to the fact he was an apostle of Jesus Christ.

Here is an excellent list of things to avoid if you want to be happy in life, but Paul had no complaint about them. They are the kind of happenings which make many people bitter. I sincerely hope I will never have as much trouble as Paul had. I do not care to be beaten, to suffer peril, to be shipwrecked, to be robbed, and certainly, to be lied about. And I don't care for forced fastings. I do not like the thought of going without meals. Along with all these troubles, Paul had the care of many churches and church troubles. No, all this is just too much!

Was all this necessary? Is all this worthwhile? No doubt, at sometime or another, all of us have come to the place of self-examination and honestly wondered whether or not it was worthwhile to continue to walk with God. Remember, you are not the first or only one to do this. Paul did it too. He checked over his life carefully. He was reckoning the future. And in so doing, he came to a very important conclusion. WHAT WAS PAUL'S CONCLUSION?

"After careful consideration and due calculation, I have reached the conclusion that the sufferings of this present time ARE NOT WORTHY TO BE COMPARED WITH THE GLORY THAT SHALL BE REVEALED IN US."

What happened to Paul to cause him to arrive at this deduction? What vision or revelation did he have? What he saw must have been tremendous.

The answer is found in the early verses of 2 Corinthians 12. Paul said,

"It is not expedient for me doubtless to glory. I will come to visions and revelations of the Lord.

(Here Paul disclosed that visions of God and revelations played a very important part in his life in determining his direction in God.)

"I knew a man in Christ above fourteen years ago, (whether in the body, I cannot tell: God knoweth;)

"How that such an one caught up to the THIRD HEAVEN.

"And I knew such a man, (whether in the body, or out of the body, I cannot tell: God knoweth;)

"How that he was caught up into PARADISE, and heard unspeakable words, which it is not lawful for a man to utter.

"Of such an one will I glory: yet of myself I will not glory, but in mine infirmities."

(v.1–5)

Paul related here an actual personal experience. It was a time when he did not know whether he was dead or alive, but God used this incident to bring him a vision of the future glory. What Paul saw was so worthy and great on the credit side of the ledger, it far outweighed all the sufferings on the debit side. The two were incomparable. The glory far outbalanced the suffering.

As we carefully study the Biblical account of the life of Paul, there is only one place where this experience could have taken place. It is reported in Acts 14.

"Let Us Make Man ... "

Paul and Barnabas arrived at the city of Lystra in Lycaonia. It was a gentile city, and like all such metropolises of the Greek world, it was given over to the worship of heathen deities. As Ephesus was the center of the worship of Diana, the supposed daughter of Venus, so Lystra was given to the worship of Jupiter, or Zeus. They believed if they gave all their worship to one god, they would be rewarded by having this same god come down into their city and walk their streets.

Here is the Bible account of the visit of Paul and Barnabas to Lystra.

"And there they preached the gospel.

"And there sat a certain man at Lystra, impotent in his feet, being a cripple from his mother's womb, who never had walked.

"The same heard Paul speak: who steadfastly beholding him, and perceiving that he had faith to be healed,

"Said with a loud voice, Stand upright on thy feet. And he leaped and walked.

"And when the people saw what Paul had done, they lifted up their voices, saying in the speech of Lycaonia, The gods are come down to us in the likeness of men.

"And they called Barnabas, Jupiter; and Paul, Mercury, because he was the chief speaker."

(Acts 14:7–12)

The news of this miracle of healing swept through the city like a fire. It reached the ears of the priest of Jupiter who tended the temple which was located at the city gates. This priest, along with the people, brought oxen and garlands (ropes of flowers), and wanted to make sacrifice to Paul and Barnabas. When the Apostles received wind of what was going on, they said, "No, you cannot do this. We are only men like you and of like passions. We are not gods."

Then the picture changed. "And there came thither certain Jews from Antioch and Iconium, who persuaded the people, and, having stoned Paul, drew him out of the city, SUPPOSING HE HAD BEEN DEAD." (Acts 14:19)

How Barnabas managed to escape from this mob we do not know. But they caught Paul, dragged him outside the city, stoned him, and left him there thinking surely he was dead.

This is the same instance which Paul related when he spoke about a man he knew about 14 years before, whether he was dead or alive, he did not know, or whether in the body, or out of the body. Paul was speaking about himself. The Lycaonians intended to do evil to Paul but this experience was turned into good by our God. Instead of dying, Paul had a vision of the Lord. He was lifted up into the third heaven, into paradise. There he saw things too glorious to tell. He heard words not lawful for him to utter. Through this experience, Paul knew a day was coming when THE GLORY OF GOD WOULD BE REVEALED THROUGH MEN. On the basis of what he saw, he came to this conclusion regarding any suffering:

"For I reckon that the sufferings of this present time ARE NOT WORTHY TO BE COMPARED

17

WITH THE GLORY WHICH SHALL BE RE-VEALED IN US."

Remember, Paul's sufferings were very real. They were not imaginary. And the glory Paul saw, which one day shall be revealed in man, is equally as real!

This glory which shall be revealed in us is described by Paul as the manifestation of the sons of God. It is so tremendous, so glorious, and so wonderful, it just cannot be placed side by side with troubles, anxieties and fears. There is absolutely no comparison between the two. The glory far outweighs the sufferings, however great they may be.

I have met many Christians who have become discouraged, heavy hearted, and out of victory in God. They seem to have lost their way and are ready to turn away from the *plow*. The reason for their discouragement is they are looking in the wrong direction. Their eyes are upon the sufferings and not the glory. And as long as they continue to view the suffering, they will not see the glory. But, once they catch a glimpse of the glory and keep their eyes upon it, the suffering loses all import!

In this book I want to emphasize the glorious future which is ours as children of God. It is my delight to constantly remind you that God is on the move. Our God has determined in His determinate counsel to bring certain things to pass and nothing can stop Him, nothing can stay His hand. God has a great plan and purpose. These shall be and along with them comes God's tremendous divine ability to "make all things work together for good." We really do not give this truth enough consideration, recognition or application. I have said it before and I will continue to say it—if God could take the cross of Jesus Christ and the terrible death He suffered at Calvary, and turn it into the salvation of the world, our God can make good to come of every problem in the life of anyone who loves Him. THIS IS THE DIVINE ABILITY OF GOD so seldom acknowledged.

Do some definite reckoning today. Look at your sufferings but do not stop there. Now compare them with what you know is yours in Christ Jesus. If you have a consciousness in your heart that you are a child of God, A GLORIOUS FUTURE IS IN STORE FOR YOU. Don't sell it short. Don't let the sufferings dim your vision.

Paul was not released from suffering just because he saw a future glory. On the contrary, it seemed the suffering was intensified. His testimony was,

> "And lest I should be exalted above measure through the abundance of the revelations, there was given to me a thorn in the flesh, the messenger of Satan to buffet me, lest I should be exalted above measure."
>
> (2 Cor. 12:7)

The Lord God desired to use Paul and He would not let Paul be ruined with pride. Spiritual pride is the archenemy of God. Scores of God's people who are suffering today have had this suffering initiated by God to keep them humble and to do them good. God has a plan to manifest Himself through men. He knows what it takes to prepare each one to make him fit to be used. James said, "Humble yourselves in the sight of the Lord, and he shall lift you up."

> (James 4:10)

TAKE YOUR EYES OFF YOURSELF. FASTEN THEM UPON THE GLORY THAT IS TO COME!

19

CHAPTER TWO

TOUCHING THE GLORY

In the epistle to the Romans, Paul said,

> "For I reckon that the sufferings of this present time are not worthy to be compared with the glory which shall be revealed in us. For the earnest expectation of the creature waiteth for the manifestation of the sons of God."
>
> (Romans 8:18,19)

The Apostle Paul had taken a careful inventory of himself—his experiences, his life and what was in his future. By weighing the sufferings he had experienced in the light of the glories he knew were to come, he concluded there was no comparison. The "sufferings were not worthy to be compared with the GLORY WHICH SHALL BE REVEALED IN US."

Please notice these words: THE GLORY WHICH SHALL BE REVEALED IN US. Here Paul is speaking about true believers in Christ, that a day is coming when God will reveal His glory through His children in a manner never before seen. Paul goes on to say that the whole of creation is waiting for this day, the day when God will manifest Himself through His sons.

21

THE MEANING OF THE PHRASE

I would like to clarify the meaning of the phrase, "the manifestation of the sons of God." First let us look closely at the word MANIFESTATION. It is derived from the Greek word, "apokalupsis", meaning, "the revelation, the revealing, or the unveiling of the sons of God". Our word has the secondary meaning, "to lighten or shine through." In other words, it is the desire of God that His children be without sin and so very transparent that He can shine through them. We are to be as vessels through whom God can "shine through." But it seems we constantly crowd out the light of God because we are prone to "love darkness rather than light."

THE BEGINNINGS

To see clearly the purposes of God in man, it is necessary for us to go back to our time of beginning which is found in the book of beginnings—the Book of Genesis.

In the first chapter, we read about the RE-CREATION OF GOD. The highlight of this re-creation was the creation of man.

"And God said, Let us make man in our image, after our likeness: and let them have dominion over the fish of the sea, and over the fowl of the air, and over the cattle, and over all the earth, and over every creeping thing that creepeth upon the earth.

"So God created man in his own image, in the image of God created he him; male and female created he them."

(Gen. 1:26,27)

After the creation of man, the Lord God brought before Adam all the rest of the creation for him to name. "And Adam gave names to all cattle, and to the fowl of the air, and to every beast of the field." And, as Adam named each one, he gained dominion over them.

But there was a major problem—Adam was lonely. Among all the creation, there was not found an helpmeet for him. So

> " ... the Lord God caused a deep sleep to fall upon Adam, and he slept: and he took one of his ribs, and closed up the flesh instead thereof;
>
> "And the rib, which the Lord God had taken from man, made he a woman, and brought her unto the man.
>
> "And Adam said, This is now bone of my bones, and flesh of my flesh: she shall be called Woman, because she was taken out of Man.
>
> "Therefore shall a man leave his father and his mother, and shall cleave unto his wife: and they shall be one flesh.
>
> "And they were both naked, the man and his wife, and were not ashamed."
>
> (Gen. 2:21–25)
>
> "The Lord God placed Adam and his wife in the garden of Eden and told them to dress it and keep it.
>
> "And the Lord God commanded the man, saying,

Of EVERY TREE of the garden thou mayest freely eat:

"But of the TREE OF THE KNOWLEDGE OF GOOD AND EVIL, thou SHALT NOT EAT of it: for in the day that thou eatest thereof thou shalt surely die."

(Gen. 2:16,17)

All was well in Eden until the day the serpent tempted Eve to disobey God. Then we are brought face to face with the fact that God and man have a common enemy. The serpent actually enticed Eve to act contrary to God's wishes. From where did this enemy come? Adam did not know he had an enemy and Eve was totally unaware that this personality wanted to ruin her and Adam's life and relationship with God. Who was this serpent?

THE ORIGINAL CREATION

For our answer, let us go back before the creation of man, back to Genesis 1:1.

The Bible begins by saying, "In the beginning God created the heaven and the earth." This is a good, clear, precise statement and all seems serene and good. Then, in verse two, the scene is changed.

"And the earth was without form, and void; and darkness was upon the face of the deep. And the Spirit of God moved upon the face of the waters."

This seems a strange way for God to make things— WITHOUT FORM, AND VOID. This means the world was

24

a WASTE, DESOLATE, EMPTY, A WRECK AND RUIN. Did God create the world a shambles or did something happen to make it that way? Are there Scriptures to throw some light upon this question? Yes. Isaiah 45:18 says,

> "For thus saith the Lord that created the heavens; God himself that formed the earth and made it; he hath established it, HE CREATED IT NOT IN VAIN, he formed it to be inhabited: I am the Lord; and there is none else."

In this verse we read words similar to Genesis 1:1. God "... formed the earth and made it; he hath established it." Now notice the next words: HE CREATED IT NOT IN VAIN, or, as translated by able Bible students, HE CREATED IT NOT A CHAOS OR WASTE. HE CREATED OR FORMED IT TO BE INHABITED.

It stands to reason then, since God did not create the world a chaos or waste, something happened to cause the world to become a chaos and a waste. That something happened between the first and second verse of Genesis 1. Does the Bible tell us what this was? Yes.

LUCIFER

God's original creation was perfect. How long it remained that way, we do not know. But from the Bible we do know that one of God's created beings was in charge of most of that creation. He was a mighty, magnificent being who governed and ruled the universe in the Name of our God.

In the original creation, before the chaos, the Lord God had many created beings to whom He had given life. These beings had ranks like an army. They had authority in their own particular rank to which they had been assigned at the time they were created. Their ranks were: (1) the anointed cherub; (2) the archangels; (3) the cherubims; (4) the seraphims; (5) principalities; (6) and powers. There may have been others, too, but of these we are certain according to the Scriptures. The Apostle Paul mentions "thrones and dominions," and these seem to relate to angelic positions.

The one angel who ruled above all others was LUCIFER. His name means, "Son of the morning," or, "Day-Star." Lucifer ruled the original creation for God. How long he ruled we do not know, but it all came to a very sudden end.

A time came when Lucifer became filled with self-importance. Because of all his power and abilities, he began to contemplate the possibility of having the sole rulership over the universe, independent of God. In fact, he decided to eliminate God entirely from the universe. In the thoughts and imaginations of Lucifer, the Creator was expendable.

With this in mind, he began a mutiny among the hosts of God. He persuaded a multitude of angelic beings to follow him and set up a revolution to overthrow the rule of God. As a result of this rebellion, the Lord God struck the material universe with a curse of judgment (which was temporary) and THE EARTH BECAME WITHOUT FORM AND VOID AND DARKNESS WAS UPON THE FACE OF THE DEEP.

In the Book of Ezekiel, chapter 28, we have an account of what happened between verse one and verse two of Genesis 1. Before we look into this important revealing chapter, I must inject some vital information regarding Bible study. First, it is a fact that the Bible interprets itself. If, in reading the Bible you come across a passage you do not understand, just hold it in abeyance and continue to read. Soon you will discover another passage which will shed light upon the first.

Another important principle of Bible study is the LAW OF DOUBLE AND TRIPLE REFERENCE. This simply means that though the Bible writers wrote to the people of their own age, their writings also are applicable to those in ages to come. In the same way, God may be speaking to a man but actually be speaking to the power governing that man. For example, when the Lord God spoke to the serpent in the garden of Eden after he had caused Adam and Eve to sin, the same words God spoke to the serpent also applied to Satan. The serpent was cursed because he allowed Satan to use him and Satan was informed at the same time of the judgment of God which would come upon him "through the seed of the woman."

This principle of double reference is found in Ezekiel 28. In the first part of the chapter, a word of the Lord is raised against a man who bears the title, The Prince of Tyre. No doubt this man was the reigning prince of Tyre during Ezekiel's day. But farther along in the same chapter (v.11), the prophet was told to "take up a lamentation upon the King of Tyrus." As far as can be determined from history, there actually was no KING of Tyrus, but there was a PRINCE. Here is an example of the Lord God speaking to Lucifer, the power behind the throne of the Prince of Tyrus and the one who had deceived him. The man was so very deceived, he said, "I am God, I sit in the seat of God." (v.2) If you are familiar with history, you know this happened many times over. Satan has been and yet is the power behind many thrones on this earth.

In the judgment of God (which is yet to come), we see the Lord Jesus dividing the nations—some are called "sheep" nations (these are those over whom God rules through a righteous ruler), and others are called "goat" nations (these are those over whom Satan rules as the power behind their

27

leaders). Here are a few of our day: Hitler in Germany; Stalin in Russia; Mao Tse Tung in China. Those who have encouraged the entrance of Red-China into the United Nations are ignorant of Bible history and the power of Satan. If they thought for one moment they were being yoked together with Satanic power by admitting Red-China, they certainly would change their minds.

When Ezekiel addressed the King of Tyrus with the word of the Lord, Ezekiel was speaking to Lucifer, the rebel, the one who caused the earth to be without form and turned into a waste. He was the power behind the throne of the Prince of Tyrus.

The words, "Thus saith the Lord God; THOU SEALEST UP THE SUM," (v.12) certainly were directed to Lucifer. It is a definite recognition of the fact that Lucifer once held the highest position in the government of God prior to his fall. Lucifer was number one—above the archangels and hosts of God, "full of wisdom, and perfect in beauty." BUT ... he was lifted up with PRIDE!

Though the Lord God desired to use Lucifer, his pride hurled him out of heaven. In these lessons we shall see again and again how it is the desire of God to use man and how easily man can fall into the same snare which caused the condemnation of the devil—pride. The Lord God will use us only as we have enough sense not to touch the glory!

In every age and generation, we have seen men rise in God and appear in the church world and then go down in a heap of ashes and broken dreams because THEY TOUCHED THE GLORY. They forgot they were only creatures, not creators. They went down because they were lifted up in pride—they touched the glory and down they went!

God has said,

"I am the Lord: that is my name: and my glory will I not give to another, neither my praise to graven images."

(Isa. 42:8)

Let me ask this question. Do you want to be used of God? If you do, why? To make a name for yourself? To have fame and position?

I have met people who desperately want the power of God in their lives but, if God gave them what they desired, they would destroy themselves. They would TOUCH THE GLORY.

Today God is preparing a people who will do the will of God without exalting themselves in pride. God WILL SHINE THROUGH humble, obedient men, but He will not share His glory with any!

Today we must analyze the powers which are motivating our lives. Who is the power in your life? Does God or Satan regulate your life? You alone can answer these questions. To pit yourself against God is disaster and ruin. Commit yourself to Him and He will shine through you.

CHAPTER THREE

LUCIFER AND AUTHORITY

The original creation of God was BEFORE the world became "without form, and void, and darkness was upon the face of the deep," as is recorded in Genesis 1:2. God did not create the heavens and the earth a chaos and a waste; this came about as a result of a catastrophic event.

In Isaiah 45:18, it is recorded,

> "For thus saith the Lord that created the heavens; God himself that formed the earth and made it: he hath established it, HE CREATED IT NOT IN VAIN, he formed it to be inhabited: I am the Lord: and there is none else."

The words of the King James Version of the Bible, "He created it not in vain," are better translated, "HE CREATED IT NOT A CHAOS OR WASTE".

The Amplified Old Testament translation says it this way:

> "For thus says the Lord Who created the heavens, God Himself Who formed the earth and made it, Who established it and created IT NOT A WORTHLESS WASTE; He formed it to be inhabited: I am the Lord, and there is no one else."

Now it stands to reason, since God did not create the heavens and the earth a chaos or waste, something transpired which caused them to become a chaos and a waste. This something took place between Genesis 1:1 and Genesis 1:2. The Bible tells us what happened.

The chaos and waste was the result of the fall of a mighty created being of the Lord, a creature named LUCIFER. His name means, "Son of the morning", or "Day-Star". He ruled for God in the original creation. A time came when Lucifer became exalted and filled with his own importance and he rebelled against God. A description of Lucifer and what brought about his fall is recorded in Ezekiel 28 and also in Isaiah 14. In this chapter we will discuss the account of Ezekiel.

We read in Ezek. 28:11,12:

> "Moreover the word of the Lord came unto me, saying, Son of man, take up a lamentation upon the king of Tyrus, and say unto him, Thus saith the Lord God: Thou sealest up the sum, full of wisdom, and perfect in beauty."

When Ezekiel addressed the words of God to the King of Tyrus, he was speaking to the power behind the earthly power addressed. He was speaking to Lucifer the rebel, the one who caused the earth to be without form and turned into a waste.

The first word of God to Lucifer was, "Thus saith the Lord God; THOU SEALEST UP THE SUM." "The full measure and pattern of exactness." (Amp.)

This statement is a recognition of the fact that Lucifer once held the highest position in the government of God.

Prior to his fall, Lucifer was the highest ranking angel. The heavens and the earth were under his dominion.

Ezekiel continued,

> "THOU HAS BEEN IN EDEN the garden of God; every precious stone was thy covering, the sardius, topaz, and the diamond, the beryl, the onyx, and the jasper, the sapphire, the emerald, and the carbuncle and gold: the workmanship of thy tabrets and of thy pipes was prepared in thee in THE DAY THAT THOU WAS CREAT-ED . . . "
>
> (v. 13)

The Eden here mentioned by Ezekiel is not the same Garden of Eden where Adam and Eve walked. That Eden was described as a garden of trees and vegetable growth. The Eden described by Ezekiel is a place of mineral beauty. The Lord God seemed very desirous to impress upon the prophet the magnificence of this great ruling angel of God.

We know without a shadow of a doubt Lucifer was a created being by these words: "The workmanship of thy tabrets and of thy pipes was prepared in thee in the day that THOU WAST CREATED." Here we learn that both Satan and evil had a beginning, and, according to the Bible, they shall have a definite end. EVIL SHALL NOT PREVAIL.

Lucifer was created in such a way that as the praises of God came through him, the sound must have been beautiful beyond comprehension as the praises were given voice through his pipes and tabrets (music). We know there was a symphony of music and praise in the beginning for the Bible tells us about it. It is recorded in Job 38:1–7.

33

"Then the Lord answered Job out of the whirlwind, and said,

"Who is this that darkeneth counsel by words without knowledge?

"Gird up now thy loins like a man; for I will demand of thee, and answer thou me.

"Where was thou when I laid the foundations of the earth? declare, if thou hast understanding.

"Who hath laid the measures thereof, if thou knowest? or who hath stretched the line upon it?

"Whereupon are the foundations thereof fastened? or who laid the cornerstone thereof.

"When the morning stars (angels) SANG TOGETHER, and all the SONS OF GOD SHOUTED FOR JOY?"

What an angelic chorus that must have been! And, thank God, when they all gather together before the throne of God, the chorus of the REDEEMED will be even greater!

Ezekiel continued to describe Lucifer. "Thou art the anointed cherub that covereth; and I have set thee so?" The Amplified renders it, "You were the anointed cherub that covers WITH OVERSHADOWING WINGS." This means Lucifer initiated and led the worship of heaven. This seems to be the ministry of the cherubs or cherubim and seraphim. We are told about them in the book of Isaiah when the prophet described his vision of the Lord. The seraphims were covering the throne of God with out-stretched wings. Isaiah said,

> "In the year that king Uzziah died I saw also the Lord sitting upon a throne, high and lifted up, and his train filled the temple.

> "Above it stood the seraphims: each one had six wings; with twain he covered his face, and with twain he covered his feet, and with twain he did fly.

> "And one cried unto another, and said, Holy, holy, holy, is the Lord of hosts: the whole earth is full of his glory."
>
> (Isa. 6:1–3)

Next we are told by Ezekiel,

> "Thou wast upon the holy mountain of God: thou hast walked up and down in the midst of the stones of fire."

Lucifer had (and fully enjoyed) a wonderful access to the throne of God. This is what it means when it says he was in the mountain of God. The term, "Thou hast walked up and down in the midst of the stones of fire," tells us he walked in the realm of God's glory. In the Scriptures we often read that the pavement under God's feet is like a devouring fire. When Moses took Aaron, Nadab, Abihu and the seventy elders of Israel up the mountain of Sinai to see the God of Israel,

35

"There was under his feet as it were a paved work
of a sapphire stone, and as it were the body of
heaven in his clearness . . . and the sight of the
glory of the Lord was like devouring fire on the top
of the mount."

(Exod. 24:10,17)

What wonder, what glory, what beautiful harmony in this
picture of the first creation of God in all its loveliness. Then
the next verse seems to close a door in our faces.

"Thou was perfect in thy ways from the day that
thou was created, till iniquity was found in thee."

(v.15)

We know these verses could not possibly have reference to
any man of Ezekiel's day because there never was a man who
was perfect in the day he was created (with the exceptions of
Adam and Jesus Christ). All of us who belong to the human
race were born in sin and shaped in iniquity. We were not
created perfect, NO NOT ONE!

In this verse we find also the perfect creation, Lucifer,
generating iniquity in his heart. Here is where sin began.
Iniquity was found in the heart of Lucifer. How could it
happen? He was a creature of tremendous power and beauty,
with all authority and wisdom. How was it possible that
iniquity should be found in him? He had all anyone could
possibly need. What more did he want? The next verse is a
great revelation.

"BY THE MULTITUDE OF THY MERCHAN-
DISE THEY HAVE FILLED THE MIDST OF
THEE WITH VIOLENCE, AND THOU HAST
SINNED."

What does this mean? Merchandise is something WHICH PASSES THROUGH THE HANDS. A merchant is one who handles goods and commodities by passing them through his hands from the wholesaler to the consumer. He does not keep them.

As the ruling angel of the Lord, much passed through the hands of Lucifer in both directions. Authority passed through him, from God to the angels of lower rank. In return, he was to carry the worship and adoration of the angelic hosts to the Eternal God. Calamity entered upon the scene when Lucifer would not allow ALL the merchandise of praise be passed through him to God. HE WANTED TO KEEP SOME FOR HIMSELF! The praise and worship was too wonderful to pass it all on to God. The authority he had felt so good, he wanted more. He had all the angels of heaven obeying the commands which God passed through him. Why not have the commands originate with himself? Why not eliminate God altogether? So Lucifer's heart was filled with the violence of rebellion.

Isn't this a terrible picture? Lucifer could not stand to "give the glory to God." He had to have some of the glory for himself.

I have met people like this. I am sure you have met them, too. At the mention of the goodness of God or what He has done for you, they become uneasy. If you testify to them how God met a financial need, they explain it away as coincidence. If you relate an experience of divine healing, they proclaim it was a natural process. No matter what is said, if the glory is given to God, they will discount it. But, should you begin to talk about them, about their abilities, their goodness or their wisdom, all rationalization stops and the glory is absorbed!

To want the glory instead of giving it to God (ALL glory

37

belongs to Him) is the bane of the Christian ministry. It seems as quickly as God begins to use someone, they become swell-headed. We seem to be able to stand most everything but blessing, authority and success. We cannot bear to just let the merchandise of praise and glory pass through us and to God. We want some of it for ourselves!

This is why God cannot use some people. He knows even a little success would be their ruin. I have met people who would give anything they possess for God's gift of healing. Why? This gift would make them big people in the ministry! They even go so far as to relate what they would do and what they would not do. God knows the heart! God knows why they desire the gift of healing—to heal the sick or to make themselves famous! GOD KNOWS OUR INNER MOTIVES. WE CANNOT FOOL HIM.

God is very careful about to whom He gives authority. Let me repeat this and emphasize it—GOD IS VERY CAREFUL ABOUT GIVING OUT AUTHORITY! This is what SONSHIP is all about. Sonship is having authority and giving God the glory. Sonship is God the Father giving authority to His children, His sons, and He does not do this indiscriminately. Those who cannot be led, receive no authority.

"For as many as are led by the Spirit of God, they are the sons of God."

(Rom. 8:14)

Some believe sonship may be attained by diligent study, by learning to quote Scriptures or by making daily affirmations concerning themselves. These do not realize that unless God can trust them to give Him the glory in the little things, they never will be trusted with greater things. These seek glory for themselves. We have a segment of superspiritual people in the country who talk about how one day they will rule with God. They talk about sitting on thrones and ruling and reigning with a rod of iron. They will tell you what is wrong with you and how right they are. The problem with most of these is they cannot rule their own spirits or their own affairs, much less have authority with God. I certainly do believe the Bible teaching that God's people will rule and reign with Him. But, if God cannot trust us now, you can be sure He will not trust us in the hereafter.

In the same way as God is careful concerning whom He gives authority, so also we must be careful in all things.

We are cautioned in the Bible to be very careful whom we select to serve in places of authority in the church. Paul cautions Timothy about giving authority and oversight—such a one must NOT BE A NOVICE. Why? "Lest being lifted up with pride he fall into the condemnation of the devil." (1 Tim. 3:6) A man must learn how to handle authority. A novice has not yet learned how to let the merchandise of God pass through his hands without wanting some of it. He is not experienced enough to know ALL the glory belongs to God.

Lucifer lost his place and his authority because he touched the glory. He was cast down. GOD COULD USE HIM NO MORE.

If you want to be used of God, WALK CAREFULLY. Be careful of pride. Don't allow yourself to become vain or puffed up. Don't fall into the same snare that condemned Lucifer. Give God all the glory!

CHAPTER FOUR

LUCIFER'S CRASH

The Bible says, "For it is God which worketh in you both to WILL and to DO of his good pleasure." (Phil. 2:13) The will of God will never be performed by any one of us unless God brings it to pass in us. By nature, all of us resist the will and purpose of God even though it be for our personal good. Why is this so? Why do we revolt against God the way we do? It is because of something which happened many ages ago. In this chapter I want to tell you about it.

Lucifer, the creature of highest rank in the original creation of God, fell from his place of authority primarily because he could not bear to rule for someone else. He could not rightly serve God because he felt he had to take the place of God, replace God, and be God himself. He touched the glory which belongs to God, and he was cast out from the mountain of God's presence. The Bible says Lucifer "was perfect in his ways from the day that he was created, till iniquity was found in him."

In this chapter we turn to the prophecy of Isaiah for insight into Lucifer's fall. We are studying carefully the account of this great angelic being and his downfall because there are important lessons here for us to learn. Lucifer had more wisdom, more knowledge, more ability, and more power than we have. Yet, he fell from the place of blessing in God. We, who are the children of God through faith in

Jesus Christ, want to be used of God and directed by Him as His sons. Therefore, we must take heed, learn our lessons well, and not miss THE MARK OF THE PRIZE OF THE HIGH CALLING OF GOD WHICH IS IN CHRIST JESUS.

In Isaiah 14:12, we read:

> "How art thou fallen from heaven, O Lucifer, son of the morning! how art thou cut down to the ground, which didst weaken the nations!"

There is little doubt who is being addressed here. It is Lucifer, the son of the morning, the one who fell from heaven.

The prophet continued,

> "For thou has said in thine heart, I will ascend into heaven, I will exalt my throne about the stars of God: I will sit also upon the mount of the congregation, in the sides of the north:

> "I will ascend above the heights of the clouds; I will be like the most High.

> "Yet thou shalt be brought down to hell, to the sides of the pit."

> (Isa. 14:12–15)

This is a clear account of the rebellion of Lucifer and the iniquity in his heart. We do not know how long God allowed the iniquity to fester in Lucifer's heart, but it was long enough for Lucifer to become thoroughly convinced he could overthrow God and have the upper hand. He was so completely sure of himself, he persuaded a third part of the angelic hosts of heaven to mutiny with him. It developed into open rebellion. And rebellion always means conflict and trouble.

Prior to this time, there was only one will dominating the universe. God's will ruled all the army of heaven. Daniel said,

> "And all the inhabitants of the earth are reputed as nothing: and HE DOETH ACCORDING TO HIS WILL IN THE ARMY OF HEAVEN, and among the inhabitants of the earth; and none can stay his hand, or say unto him, What doest thou?"
> (Dan. 4:35)

Before Lucifer's rebellion, the armies of heaven obeyed one will—the will of God. And the armies of heaven, since Lucifer's fall, continue to obey one will—the will of God. In fact, we are taught in the Lord's prayer to pray on this wise, "Thy kingdom come, thy WILL BE DONE, ON EARTH, as IT IS IN HEAVEN." Yes, there is coming a day when the will of God will be the only will here on earth, just as it NOW IS IN HEAVEN. This is the only way there will ever be peace and rest for every man's soul.

With Lucifer's rebellion and the agitation it created, there seemingly were two courses open to God.

1. To completely destroy and annihilate Lucifer.

2. To replace Lucifer with another creature and allow Lucifer to run his course and show to all history, openly and concisely, that rebellion against God is rebellion against one's self in the end.

If you are familiar with the Bible, you know God chose the latter course. God is permitting Lucifer (Satan) to infest the

43

world with evil and war against the minds of men in an attempt to bring them into captivity to do his will. But through it all, God is preparing a people who will delight to do the will of God. These, whom He calls His sons, He will lead into glory. And that glory will be a position far higher than any position known by Lucifer.

Before we go farther, I want to take time to carefully consider the rebellion of Lucifer, and what he had decided in his heart. In Isaiah 14, we have five statements made by Lucifer, each one stating, "I will." Let us examine them.

1. I WILL ASCEND INTO HEAVEN

This is an indication that the rebellion of Lucifer began here on this earth. Genesis 1:1 says, "In the beginning God created the heaven and the earth." We must remember that this earth of ours is the center of God's attention. This is His stage. This is the planet where He has put life.

Often I am asked if I believe there is intelligent life on other planets. To this I answer, "No." I believe the angelic hosts of God inhabit the heavens, but as far as a race of men to threaten us with flying saucers from another planet, this I do not believe. The reason for my strong assertion is that the Bible teaches many things found here on earth were made after a pattern of things in the heavens which were there before God ever created the heavens and the earth. We are told of a tabernacle which Moses was instructed to build. The pattern for this earthly building was the true tabernacle which already existed in the heavens. When Jesus died, He died for the souls of men here on this earth, and after His burial and resurrection, He ascended into heaven itself to appear in the true tabernacle on our behalf.

Lucifer, at least, must have had full access to the primal earth, for he said in his heart, "I will ascend into heaven." This means he intended to go up! If he did not inhabit the

44

earth, then it does not seem reasonable God should have turned the earth into a chaos and waste. The Bible says, "The earth was without form and void," not the heavens!

Secondly, we must remember that the primal earth must have existed for thousands of years prior to the fall of Lucifer, many ages before the re-creation and the creation of Adam and Eve. This accounts for the age of our earth as estimated by our scientists. The Bible does not teach the world was created five days prior to the creation of Adam and Eve. The Bible distinctly teaches of a world that was, and a world that is now. Peter writes about this in 2 Peter 3:5–7:

"By the Word of God the heavens were of old, and the earth standing out of the water and in the water:

"Whereby the world that THEN WAS, being overflowed with water, perished:

"But the heavens and the earth, which ARE NOW, by the same word are kept in store, reserved unto fire against the day of judgment and perdition of ungodly men."

If this truth were taught to all our youth, they clearly would know the Bible teachings about our beginnings—the world that was and the world that now is. This reconciles the Bible and science as to the age of our earth.

2. I WILL EXALT MY THRONE ABOVE THE STARS OF GOD.

Throughout the Word of God, the term "stars" is used to denote the "messengers" of the Lord. It is used also to denote angels who in reality are God's messengers. So, when Lucifer said, "I will exalt my throne above the STARS of God," he was denoting a place above the angels of God.

But even this position was not high enough for Lucifer. He wanted more!

3. I WILL SIT ALSO UPON THE MOUNT OF THE CONGREGATION, IN THE SIDES OF THE NORTH.

In this statement, Lucifer aspired to government. He wanted the seat of goverment and authority over all the hosts of God. What arrogance! When he spoke of the "sides of the north," he spoke of the location of the seat of government. In studying the Bible carefully, we find the governmental seat of God is designated to be in the north. In any case, Lucifer stated the intention of his will.

We are told that the mind and will are actuated by motives. Notice carefully what set into motion the "I wills" of Lucifer—the motive of pride!

4. I WILL ASCEND ABOVE THE HEIGHTS OF THE CLOUDS.

In the Bible, clouds usually refer to the GLORY OF GOD. A cloud of God's presence went before Israel in their journey through the desert. The cloud of God's presence came down into the tabernacle of Moses and covered the Holy Place. When Christ ascended into heaven, the cloud of God's presence bore Him away. Clouds are a symbol of the glory of God, even the very throne of heaven. This is the place to which Satan aspired to mount!

It is surprising how men want to take away the glory of God. Of Israel, David said, "They changed their glory into the similitude of an ox that eateth grass." (Psa. 106:20) As men, they knew they were made in the image of God, but they deliberately made the image of God look like a beast.

5. I WILL BE LIKE THE MOST HIGH.

When Lucifer said in his heart, "I will be like the most High," he was actually saying, "I will be EL ELYON." This was the name by which God revealed Himself to Abraham when Abraham was blessed by the king-priest Melchizedek. It means literally, THE POSSESSOR OF HEAVEN AND EARTH.

Lucifer's rebellion was not a request for God to move over and share His throne; it was a threat to remove God entirely from the throne. This was open war. It was an attempt to put God out so Satan could take His place as "possessor of heaven and earth."

Lucifer did not succeed in his plan. God cast him out of the heavens. Instead of ascending, he started on a long descent!

What do the children of God learn from this? We learn if WE EXALT OURSELVES, WE WILL BE ABASED. Self-exaltation and pride are ruinous to anyone. God cannot and will not use a man who thinks more highly of himself than he ought to think.

"Humble yourselves in the sight of the Lord, and he shall lift you up."

(Jas. 4:10)

The Bible goes further to say,

"God resisteth the proud, but giveth grace to the humble."

(Jas. 4:6)

Pride, arrogance, self-will, turned the greatest of the arch-angels into the devil. Such traits always have the same

47

results. If you want to be used of God, get your ego under control. It is the meek and the humble who will inherit the earth. Shrink your head to fit the size of your hat. God does not exalt the arrogant. He brings them down with a terrible crash. ASK LUCIFER. HE KNOWS!

CHAPTER FIVE

ORDER OUT OF CHAOS

Thus far we have learned a number of very important truths. By vision and by revelation, the Apostle Paul saw a great and tremendous future for the children of God which he called "The Manifestation of the Sons of God." He further stated, the problems of today and the sufferings of this present time do not deserve to be compared with the glory that is to be revealed in the children of God. The Apostle said it this way,

"For I reckon that the sufferings of this present time are not worthy to be compared with the glory which shall be revealed in us.

"For the earnest expectation of the creature waiteth for the manifestation of the sons of God."
(Rom. 8:18,19)

We also learned why this manifestation was necessary. In the Genesis account of the creation, the testing, and the fall of our first parents, Adam and Eve, we saw they had an enemy about whom they apparently knew nothing. That enemy, speaking through the serpent, beguiled Eve into thinking the Lord God was withholding something good from her and her husband. She was deceived in her thinking. Through deception, Adam openly defied God and trans-gressed His command.

"Let Us Make Man . . . "

Our study carried us into an investigation of this enemy of Adam and Eve. He was a creature of God who once had been "the anointed cherub of God who had covered the very throne of the Eternal with his outstretched wings." This anointed cherub was named Lucifer, which means "Day-Star, or the star of the morning."

Lucifer had once been a blessed subject of God. His start was as the prince on earth and seemingly he ruled over the creation of God. One of his chief duties was to enter into heaven to carry the worship of his principality into the presence of God, even into the very throne room of heaven. So great was the power of Lucifer exercised on earth, he determined to move into heaven and also take possession of its government.

Lucifer said in his heart,

> "I will ascend into heaven. I will exalt my throne above the stars of God. I will sit upon the mount of the congregation, in the sides of the north. I will ascend above the heights of the clouds. I will be like the Most High."
>
> (Isa. 14:13,14)

However, his ambitions were not to be realized, for the Lord God said, "Yet thou shalt be brought down to hell, to the sides of the pit."

> (Isa. 14:15)

Lucifer, who became Satan, lusted in his heart for that which was not rightfully his, and he lost his place in the economy of God. His ambition made him the devil. The lust for power and things which are not lawful had made the earth the hell it is. In fact, the Bible says all the corruption in the world is the result of lust. Peter said,

50

"Whereby are given unto us exceeding great and precious promises: that by these ye might be partakers of the divine nature, having escaped the CORRUPTION that is in the world THROUGH LUST."

(2 Peter 1:4)

Translated literally, this would read, "Having escaped the corruption that is in the world THROUGH WANTING ONE'S OWN WAY . . ."

This is exactly the cause of Lucifer's downfall. HE WANTED HIS OWN WAY! There is little doubt this same thing also can be the ruination of anyone of us. Bascially we all want our own way.

When Lucifer wanted his own way (instead of the will and way of God), he introduced a CONTRARY WILL into the universe. And, whenever one will is set contrarily and arbitrarily against another, agitation, conflict and war is the result. This is precisely what happened. But the Lord God did not sit back and ignore this contrariness. That rebellion had to be judged.

Two paths of action were avilable to God:

(1) He could destroy Satan with the Word of His mouth.

(2) He could allow Satan and evil to run its course, and thereby show to all His creatures throughout time and history that rebellion against God brings judgment, that only in the will of God can true happiness and fulfillment be found.

It is quite evident, from the Bible record, the course the Lord God took. HE DID NOT DESTROY SATAN (of this there is little doubt), but He did destroy the domain of Satan. The material world was blasted into a chaos by the firey indignation that proceeded out of the mouth of God. THE EARTH BECAME WITHOUT FORM, AND VOID. The

"Let Us Make Man ... "

Prophet Jeremiah described it as God enabled him to look back into history. He said,

> "I beheld the earth, and, lo, it was without form, and void; and the heavens, and they had no light. I beheld the mountains, and, lo, they trembled, and all the hills moved lightly. I beheld, and, lo, there was no man, and all the birds of the heavens were fled. I beheld, and, lo, the fruitful place was a wilderness, and all the cities thereof were broken down at the presence of the Lord, and by HIS FIERCE ANGER."
>
> (Jer. 4:23–26)

We know from science, violent convulsions must have taken place upon the earth, for it was covered with the waters of the oceans. The sun was extinguished, the stars could not be seen, and the clouds descended upon the earth's surface. Not a living thing could be found on the whole planet. The shutting off of the light of the sun no doubt caused the moisture and waters of the earth to freeze. The earth became covered with vast glaciers of ice. The geologists tell us there are marks of these glaciers all over the earth, even in the center of equatorial Africa.

God judged; God spoke; and the earth had become an enormous RUIN. BUT GOD DID NOT GO OUT OF BUSINESS. GOD DID NOT DESERT THE EARTH. The Bible record says: "And the SPIRIT OF GOD moved upon the face of the waters." (Gen. 1:2)

Perhaps, in your imagination, you can, in some way, conceive what this must have been like. Lucifer, who thought he could take the place of God, now roamed around in the ruined universe, brooding, sulking, and filling himself with hatred against God. I am quite sure there must have been occasions when his deluded heart was so filled with visions of his power and grandeur, he endeavored to bring some order out of this terrible chaos. I can picture him shouting up and down the earth, "Let there be light... Let there be light!" But after the echo of his voice died, nothing remained but silence and darkness. Lucifer could not create. He was not the creator; HE WAS A CREATURE. He had reached for the brass ring and had missed!

Just how long Lucifer roamed through the chaotic universe we are not sure, but it well could have been millions of years. Whatever the theory as to primeval time, it can be fitted into the vastness of the Genesis record.

GOD'S INTERVENTION

What Satan could not do even in ages, the Lord God did with a single word. He said, "Let there be light: AND THERE WAS LIGHT." (Gen. 1:3) Our God began to speak. The silence of millions of years was broken. Ten times in the first chapter of Genesis we find the phrase: "AND GOD SAID." Here is the order of the RE-CREATION.

THE FIRST DAY: The appearance of light and the separation of the light from the darkness; the orderliness of day and night.

THE SECOND DAY: The firmament, or atmosphere which we breathe was formed. By its insertion the waters which float above the earth were again raised to their place, separated from those which are upon the earth.

THE THIRD DAY: The voice of the Lord was again heard. In quick response, the whole planet resounded with the roar of rushing floods as the waters were gathered into their proper places and the dry land appeared.

"And God called the dry land Earth; and the

gathering together of the waters called He Seas: and God saw that it was good."

(Gen. 1:10)

On the same day the Word of God went forth a second time. The earth became covered with a garment of vegetation—grass, herbs, flowers, trees. Everything had seed within itself, so it could reproduce after its kind.

THE FOURTH DAY: God now began a work in the heavens also by the Word of His mouth. He said:

"Let there be lights in the firmament of the heaven to divide the day from the night; and let them be for signs, and for seasons, and for days, and years: and let them be for lights in the firmament of the heaven to give light upon the earth: and it was so. And God made two great lights; the greater light to rule the day, and the lesser light to rule the night: he made the stars also."

(Gen. 1:14–16)

The heavens definitely were made and have a special relationship to our earth.

THE FIFTH DAY: Now that the habitat of earth and heavens were prepared, the creative power of God was put forth, and the waters, which had been void of living beings, were commanded to swarm with the creature that hath life. Fowls were created to fly through the heavens.

"And God blessed them, saying, Be fruitful, and multiply, and fill the waters in the seas, and let fowl multiply in the earth."

(Gen. 1:22)

And sea and air were filled with life.

THE SIXTH DAY: The making of man.

> "And God said, Let us make man in our image,
> after our likeness: and let them have domin-
> ion . . . "

(Gen. 1:26)

In Exodus 20:11, we read,

> "For in six days the Lord made heaven and earth,
> the sea and all that in them is."

Notice carefully the Bible says God MADE these things in six days. It does not say He "CREATED" them. There is a difference. The verb CREATE is used for origination. "In the beginning God CREATED . . ." The verbs used in the account of the six days contain no concept of creation. These words have to do with the arranging and ordering of existing materials into new forms. "God divided . . . God made . . . God gathered . . . God set . . ." The Bible teaches that the perfect, created world was blasted to ruin and desolation. Afterward it was re-formed and re-fashioned in the six days of the Genesis record. God did not destroy the entire earth at the time of Lucifer's revolt because God had a PLAN for the earth.

THE PLACE OF DOMINION

After the Lord God had re-formed and re-fashioned the earth, it was necessary for Him to place someone in the sphere of dominion; someone who would rule for Him. One would think after the fall of Lucifer, the "anointed cherub",

55

one of the archangels would be next in line for dominion. We read in the Bible about the great archangels Gabriel and Michael. Surely one of these would have the place of dominion.

I have given this idea considerable thought. I wonder if this matter of dominion was not the subject of much consideration among the angelic hosts of God. During the years and ages that Lucifer roamed through the darkness of this world, I am sure there must have been some speculation as to who would take his place in the government of the principality that was known as the earth. And it must have been quite a surprise to all the hosts of heaven when the Lord God bypassed them all and said,

> "let us make man in our image, after our likeness: AND LET THEM HAVE DOMINION . . . "

These words not only startled the angels but have been a source of wonderment to thinking men and women down through the ages. David said,

> "When I consider thy heavens, the work of thy fingers, the moon and the stars, which thou hast ordained; (I say) What is man, that thou art mindful of him? and the son of man, that thou visitest him?

> "For thou hast made him a LITTLE LOWER THAN THE ANGELS, and hast CROWNED him with glory and honour.

> "THOU MADEST HIM TO HAVE DOMINION

OVER THE WORKS OF THY HANDS; thou
hast put all things under his feet."

(Psa. 8:3–6)

From these words of David we see God had a tremendous
purpose in the creation of man and setting him in the place
of dominion.

I am sure you can appreciate the fact that Lucifer, who
became Satan and dwelt here on this earth, knew what the
Lord God said when He made man. There is little doubt
Satan retaliated, "Man shall not have dominion . . . THIS IS
MINE. The glory and honor of ruling this earth is mine,
NOT MAN'S." So a bitter conflict started between Satan
and man. Satan plotted the overthrow of man. His determi-
nation was and has been, "Man will not rule me: I will rule
man!"

Let's bring this down to present day reality. How do things
stand with you? Do you have dominion over Satan, or does
he have dominion over you?

Be honest in your answer!

CHAPTER SIX

THE STRUGGLE FOR DOMINION

In Genesis 1:26, the Bible states,

> "And God said, Let us make man in our image, after our likeness: and let them have dominion over the fish of the sea, and over the cattle, and OVER ALL THE EARTH, and over every creeping thing that creepeth upon the earth. So God created man in his own image, in the image of God created he him; male and female created he them."

In our last chapter we learned man was placed in the position of dominion over the re-formed earth. This must have been a source of wonderment to the angelic hosts of heaven. When the Lord God re-formed and re-fashioned the earth, it was necessary for Him to put someone in charge, someone who would rule for Him. After the fall of Lucifer, "the anointed cherub", it seemed certain one of the archangels would be the successor for dominion. We read about the great archangels, Gabriel and Michael. Surely, they would be in line for authority. However, this was not the case. The Lord God did not choose an angel to rule the earth. He stated He would bring into being a NEW creation, a creation called MAN, who would have dominion over ALL the earth.

The comprehension of much of the rest of the Bible and of

the plan and purpose of God, depends upon understanding the position of man in the ranks of God's created beings. When the Lord God created the angelic beings, He established them in an orderly hierarchy. Lucifer (as we have seen in our previous studies) was created the highest angelic being of all. There was no creature superior to him. Under his rule were all the varied orders of the angelic creation: cherubs, seraphs, the archangels, principalities, powers, thrones, dominions and lower angels.

But when the Almighty moved to create MAN, He did not use any of the angelic orders as the pattern. God said, "Let us make man in OUR IMAGE, AFTER OUR LIKENESS." Always remember this!

Next we learn man was NOT given the same power as Lucifer had. He was not given the authority over angelic beings who were called "principalities and powers" nor was man given the ability possessed by the angels to move through the air and heavens with great speed and freedom of movement. Man was confined to the earth. The Bible clearly states, when God made man, HE MADE HIM A LITTLE LOWER THAN THE ANGELS. David said,

> "When I consider the heavens, the work of thy fingers, the moon and the stars, which thou has ordained; (I say), What is man that thou art mindful of him? and the son of man, that thou visitest him? For thou HAST MADE HIM A LITTLE LOWER THAN THE ANGELS, and has crowned him with glory and honour."
>
> (Psa. 8:3–5)

God created man below ALL the angelic orders and fastened him to the earth with the law of gravity, limiting him in space, in time, in intelligence, and in power. God has a plan to bring up from the lowest of the creation, THOSE WHO WILL RULE THE UNIVERSE WITH HIM. The Lord God will show even to principalities and powers, that He will exalt whomsoever He will, and that all things work according to the WILL and PURPOSE OF THE ALMIGHTY.

When the Lord God created man and gave him DOMINION, there must have been an instant awareness in the mind of Satan that man was his rival. Now Satan had an opponent. You can imagine what went on in the mind of Satan. You can imagine how he set about with schemes and plans. He had been nursing resentment and hatred against God for ages. Now God put a competitor into the ring with him! He probably said with himself and to his legions of demons, "If this man thinks he will have dominion over me, he has another thought coming! The Almighty does not rule me. Does man think he can rule me?"

I suppose you are probably also wondering about this. From the looks of things, Satan seems to have a definite advantage. He is a much higher creation than man. He has more power and more authority. How can man possibly come out on top? The answer; GOD MADE MAN IN HIS IMAGE AND IN HIS LIKENESS. There is more to this statement than first meets the eye. This truth we will consider in detail later, but now let us continue with the first confrontation of man and Satan.

Please keep in mind, when God made Adam he must have been a splendid being. Science tells us all that man is today was handed down to him genetically through his genes. The genes of the human race carry in them all the human traits and talents. When we analyze the talents of such brilliant men as Shakespeare, Plato, Beethoven, Michaelangelo, Isaac Newton, and Albert Einstein, we wonder what Adam was really like. He must have been a magnificent specimen. For, in the loins of Adam were the genes which contained all the traits and talents passed down to the human race. Imagine, all the genius of the race contained in one man!

THE MEETING

Now let us consider the meeting of man and Satan. Before the fall, after the creation of Adam, man was alone. The Lord God brought the creation before Adam

> "to see what he would call them: and whatsoever Adam called every living creature, that was the name thereof. And Adam gave names to all cattle, and to the fowl of the air, and to every beast of the field; but for Adam there was not found an helpmeet for him. And the Lord God caused a deep sleep to fall upon Adam, and he slept: and he took one of his ribs, and closed up the flesh instead thereof; and the rib, which the Lord God had taken from man, made he a woman, and brought her unto the man. And Adam said, This is now bone of my bone, and flesh of my flesh: she shall be called Woman, because she was taken out of Man. Therefore shall a man leave his father and his mother, and shall cleave unto his wife: and they shall be one flesh."
>
> (Gen. 2:19–24)

God placed the man, Adam, and the woman, Eve, in a garden eastward in Eden. They were told to dress it and keep it. They were also told,

> "Of every tree of the garden thou mayest eat: But of the tree of the knowledge of good and evil, thou

shalt not eat of it: for in the day that thou eatest
thereof you shalt surely die."

(Gen. 2:16,17)

God gave man dominion over all the earth and its creatures. He could eat freely of every tree in the garden with just
one exception. He was commanded NOT to eat of the fruit
of the tree of the knowledge of good and evil.

I am asked quite often if I believe this story in literal.
"Surely, you do not believe that story and think the trans-
gression of Adam was the eating of a piece of fruit!" Yes, I
believe it was a matter just as simple as that! The fruit he ate
was unimportant; the obedience test was the important
thing. They had a restriction placed upon them by God and
they were to learn obedience to Him. THEY WERE TO
OBEY GOD!

Down through history, people have endeavored to make
this fruit of the knowledge of good and evil every conceivable thing. In our day, some teach that the forbidden fruit was
sex. This idea began centuries ago with Roman Catholic
theologians and it has continued to be propagated to every
generation. This theory is silly and preposterous, to say the
least. There is, of course, no sin whatsoever in the marital
relationship which God declares to have created as an
illustration of the oneness and union of the church with the
Lord Jesus Christ.

(Eph. 5:32)

When Satan set out to ruin Adam, his strategy was to
entice the man to declare his independence from God. The
fruit of the tree of the knowledge of good and evil was a sign
that Adam was in a place of submission.

The Bible record continues,

63

"Let Us Make Man . . . "

"Now the serpent was more subtile than any beast of the field which the Lord God had made. And he said unto the woman, Yea, hath God said, Ye shall not eat of every tree of the garden?"

The answer of Eve was:

"We may eat of the fruit of the trees of the garden: But of the fruit of the tree which is in the midst of the garden, God hath said, Ye shall not eat of it, neither shall ye touch it, lest ye die."

(Gen. 3:2,3)

Satan, speaking through the serpent, repudiated God's word.

"Ye shall not surely die: for God doth know that in the day ye eat thereof, then your eyes shall be opened, and ye shall be as gods, knowing good and evil."

(Gen. 3:4,5)

Satan was enticing Eve to detach herself from the Word of God. She began to think:

"God has been lying to us. If we eat of this fruit we will not die; we will be as gods. The Lord God doesn't want us to be like him. He is deceiving us. If we eat of the fruit we will know good and evil for ourselves, and can declare our independence from God."

And when the woman saw that the tree was good for food,

and that it was pleasant to the eye, and a tree to be desired to make one wise, she took of the fruit thereof, and did eat, and gave also unto her husband with her; and he did eat." (Gen. 3:6)

Here are the words which brought the judgment of God upon Adam, "AND HE DID EAT!" Adam deliberately transgressed against the Word of God. This is what Satan had hoped for. Satan, who did not know the wisdom of God, was using creature logic. He reasoned since God has blasted him for rebellion, He would do the same to Adam. Satan, by the time of the fall, knew the nature of God, that God was forced to strike sin in its every appearance. So, when God created man, Satan's thought was to seduce him from God in order to have one more creature under his sway and to frustrate the plan of God in the bargain.

But God's plans cannot be frustrated. Satan has wisdom that is greater than human wisdom but which is still folly in comparison with the wisdom of God. Satan's logic was: "If I can succeed in detaching man from God, then God, by His nature, will have to curse man. In this way my rule over the sphere of the earth will not be disturbed."

But, to his utter consternation, Satan saw God coming with a pleading call of love, seeking the erring man and woman. That must have been one of the most startling moments in Satan's history. Instead of striking out as lightning, the Lord God of creation came down to the garden in the cool of the day and called, "Adam, where art thou?"

Satan, of course, was correct in assuming that God must blast all sin. But, not knowing the plan of God, he didn't realize the God of judgment is also a God of grace and mercy. There was a judgment upon the ground, a judgment upon the animals of the earth, and a certain change in the man and the woman, but God continued to deal with them in grace. He took the fig leaves from them and covered them with coats of skins, and continued a fellowship with them in spite of the judgment.

Through the disobedience of Adam, a curse came upon the whole of creation. Paul said to the Romans,

> "for the creature (creation) was made subject to vanity (emptiness, futility) not willingly, but by reason of him who hath subjected the same in hope."
>
> (Rom. 8:20)

Satan had hoped he could plunge the re-fashioned earth of God under judgment and so cause the plan and program of God to come to naught. Adam subjected the entire creation to the curse of God by hoping he could be a god and rule the creation independently of the Lord. Both Satan and Adam ended up in futility for neither of their hopes were realized. Only God, in the last analysis, gained a victory. God was yet going to have His way.

Think of the sorrow Adam brought upon the human race through his rebellion and self-will. He had no idea of the consequences of sin-sickness-infirmity, and death—but they came. And, remember, these problems all come as a result of rebellion against God. But, in spite of the rebellion, we know God still cares. God knows the world is in a terrible condition and He has the power to alter it. But He is waiting patiently and working steadily to bring about His eternal purposes IN AND THROUGH MAN.

CHAPTER SEVEN

THE DECLARATION OF WAR

We have reached the point in our study where Adam, the first man, deliberately transgressed against the command of God. Eve was deceived by Satan speaking to her through the serpent. The Bible narrative says:

> "And when the woman saw that the tree was good for food, and that it was pleasant to the eyes, and a tree to be desired to make one wise, she took of the fruit thereof, and did eat, and gave also unto her husband with her; and he did eat."
>
> (Gen. 3:6)

These are the words which brought the judgment of God upon Adam, AND HE DID EAT! Adam deliberately transgressed against the Word of God. This was exactly what Satan hoped for. It looked like certain victory for Satan so he could again be in the place of dominion over the earth.

By Adam's sin, sin entered into the world of man. And through sin came death. Romans 5:12, says,

> "Wherefore, as by one man sin entered into the world, and death by sin; and so death passed upon all men, for that all have sinned."

Death came into the world by the sin of one man, Adam.

Notice carefully, sin and death did not come into the world through the sin of Eve. Nowhere in the Bible is the woman blamed for the death which came upon the race. Nowhere in the Bible is the woman blamed for the fall or its consequences. In fact, the New Testament flatly states,

> "Adam was formed first, then Eve: and Adam was not deceived, but the woman was deceived."
>
> (I Tim. 2:14)

This is a most important point in the Biblical doctrine of the entrance of sin into the world.

If Adam had sinned before Eve, the fall of the race would not have been complete and Eve would have had a perfect excuse before God. If God asked her to explain her actions, she could have answered, "I have done exactly what I was told to do. I have obeyed my husband and followed his example." This was not the case. The sin which caused the ruin of the race was willful, determined rebellion on the part of Adam.

It was not enough for man to have everything with just one exception. He immediately wanted the one exception! He deliberately rebelled against the Word of God.

From this point and on through history, man has been out of right relation with God. Everywhere, in the Bible, he is revealed as a rebel against God, his nature of corruption and depravity hardening and deepening as time goes on. Within a comparatively brief period after the fall, it was necessary for God to destroy the human race except for Noah and his family, because of Satanic possession which had rapidly enveloped mankind.

> "And God saw that the wickedness of man was great in the earth, and that every imagination of

the thoughts of his heart was only evil continually."

(Gen. 6:5)

Read David's description of humanity.

"The Lord looks down from heaven upon the
children of men, to see if there are any that act
wisely, that seek after God. (The conclusion:)
They have all gone astray, they are all alike
corrupt; there is none that does good, no, not one.

(Psa. 14:2,3)

Isaiah has the same view:

"The whole head is sick, and the whole heart faint.
From the sole of the foot even to the head there is
no soundness in it, but wounds, and bruises and
putrifying sores: they have not been closed, nor
bound up, or softened with ointment."

(Isa. 1:5,6)

According to Jeremiah,

"The heart (of man) is deceitful above all things
and incurably wicked."

(Jer. 17:9)

Because Adam sinned, God had to act. Failure to punish
such arrogant presumption would mean God was no longer
in control. God must act; and act He did. According to His
righteousness and holiness God SEPARATED THE SIN-
NER, ADAM, FROM HIMSELF. This separation meant
death.

69

The chief characteristic of death is separation. When a person dies physically, there is a separation of the soul and spirit from the body. When life ends, the soul leaves the body, taking the spirit with it. As a result, the body quickly begins to decay. Death has set in. This is a picture of the greater separation which took place when sin entered into the world. Man's soul and spirit were separated, not from the body, but FROM GOD.

When Adam sinned, he fell into SPIRITUAL DARK-NESS. Though Adam was still very much alive physically, SPIRITUAL LIFE WAS GONE. When the moment came for him to face God, he fled in terror to hide among the trees. He feared to meet God who had so generously provided for him and whom he had disobeyed. Sin had done its work of separation. Man's fellowship with his Creator was broken. Now Adam feared to face God.

This is why men fear physical death. Engraved into our very innermost being is the knowledge that, when death comes, we will have to face God. And to face God unprepared, is a frightening thought to any man, regardless of who he is.

SATAN'S MISCALCULATION

Man had sinned and Satan waited for the God of righteousness and justice to destroy Adam and Eve, and the rest of the creation. But, as Satan waited, he heard something he did not expect to hear. He heard the voice of God in Eden say to Adam,

"Adam, where art thou?"

(Gen. 3:9)

Adam's answer was,

70

"I heard thy voice in the garden, and I was afraid, because I was naked; and I hid myself."

The Lord said,

"Who told thee that thou wast naked? Hast thou eaten of the tree, whereof I commanded thee that thou shouldest not eat?"

Adam, who aspired to be a god by declaring his independence from God, became a cowering coward and liar. He shunned the blame that was rightfully his by saying,

"The woman whom thou gavest to be with me, she gave me of the tree, and I did eat."

Adam is laying the blame to Eve, but, actually, he is holding God responsible for the whole thing. It was God's fault Eve was around! If God had not given him that woman, he would have been all right!

The Lord God then turned to the woman and said,

"What is this that thou hast done?"

In answer, Eve followed the cowardly example of her husband by shifting the blame to the serpent.

"The serpent beguiled me, and I did eat."

In the answers of Adam and Eve we see the deceitfulness of sin. They were lying to themselves and to God. They began to practice deceit and "buck-passing" the moment they stepped out of the will of God and began to exercise their own will.

The Lord God then turned to the serpent and said, "Because thou hast done this, thou art cursed above all cattle, and above every beast of the field; upon thy belly shalt thou go, and dust shalt thou eat all the days of thy life."

Then, while speaking to the serpent, the Lord God suddenly addressed Satan, the power behind the actions of the serpent.

> "And I will put enmity between thee and the woman, and between thy seed and her seed; it shall bruise thy head, and thou shalt bruise his heel."
>
> (Gen. 3:15)

This was something Satan did not bargain for. He had expected to have a confederate by getting Adam to rebel against God. Now, instead of having a confederate, the Lord said He would put ENMITY between man and Satan. Satan did not know the wisdom of God. Upon this fact rests our entire understanding of God's plan—GOD HAS PUT AN ENMITY BETWEEN MAN AND SATAN. By nature, man and Satan are NOT workers together; each is working for himself, to accomplish his own ends!

Enmity means: hatred, rancor, mutual antagonism, and mutual hostility.

The Lord God decreed there would be a hatred between Satan and man. God, Himself, would put it there. As a result of this hatred and rancor, the day would come when the seed of the woman would BRUISE the head or governmental power of Satan, and Satan, in turn, would bruise the heel of man.

Here God actually pronounced a coming doom upon

Satan which would take place through the seed of the woman. Now, it stands to reason, since Satan now knew he was to be defeated and destroyed by means of a child born of woman, he immediately set out to guard against the eventuality by seeking to destroy this seed in whatever family it might appear.

The first guess of Satan was that Abel was that man. He watched closely for an occasion to attack Abel. This Satan managed through Abel's brother, Cain. Notice carefully how the opportunity presented itself.

A close examination of the story reveals God had commanded both Cain and Abel to bring a blood sacrifice. Though not stated in the Book of Genesis, we read in Hebrews that by faith, Abel offered unto God a more excellent sacrifice than Cain. (Heb. 11:4) Since Abel acted in faith, it is certain he was moving according to a command of God. Abel bowed before God, acknowledged his need, and accepted the provision made for him by the grace of God. Cain resented this symbol of dependency upon God. He refused to bring the designated offering and, unable to strike God Himself, vented his rage on his innocent brother. But before Cain slew Abel, he deliberately sinned against God, and Satan took occasion by this. If Cain had not sinned against God, he never would have murdered Abel. Satan saw the rebellion in Cain, reasoned Cain was not the promised seed but Abel, and, therefore, prompted Cain to kill Abel.

From this point, Satan blindly attempted to destroy all men that he surely might blot out the line of the promise. But, Satan eventually discovered there were certain men who had been chosen by God for an eternal purpose. So his hatred was concentrated upon these. We see this hatred turned against the Nation of Israel, against the prophets, and against every man who was truly chosen of God.

Satan hates anyone who walks close to the Lord. Jesus said,

> "And ye shall be hated of ALL MEN for my name's sake; but he that endureth to the end shall be saved."
>
> (Mt. 24:9)

Satan prompted men to kill every prophet the Lord God sent in his attempt to destroy the promised seed who would eventually destroy him. Satan exerts a HATRED (enmity) AGAINST EVERY TRUE CHILD OF GOD. Satan hates God and all who are BORN OF GOD. Satan had grounds for hating mankind, because he knew not which new child might be the seed which would bruise his power. He further had grounds for a jealous hatred because God, periodically through the prophets, announced that all the glories and functions which once belonged to Lucifer would be given to mankind through the coming of the promised seed. The Lord God announced He would ultimately have a group of called-out people whom He would call His sons, the church, and He would make them the successors of Satan in every realm.

Paul the Apostle, declared this has been the plan of God since he first formed man. It was Paul's calling to

> " ... make all men see what is the fellowship of the mystery, which from the beginning of the world hath been hid in God, who created all things by Jesus Christ: to the intent that now unto the PRINCIPALITIES AND POWERS IN HEAVENLY PLACES might be known by the church the MANIFOLD WISDOM OF GOD."
>
> (Eph. 3:9,10)

74

God has always had a purpose in man. Satan has always purposed to kill and stamp it out. When the Lord Jesus Christ was born, Satan's hatred came to a white heat. Satan moved upon Herod to kill all babies under two years of age, according to the time which he had diligently inquired of the wise men. But God had arranged an escape in advance. The wise men brought gifts of gold to the family of Jesus to make it possible for them to escape into Egypt. Jesus grew up before the Father as a "tender plant" and the Almighty would not allow Him to be touched until His own designated time and place. That time and place was Calvary when the "fullness of time" had come.

For if the prince of this world, Satan, had known the wisdom of God,

> " . . . he would not have crucified the Lord of Glory."
>
> (I Cor. 2:7,8)

This was the beginning of the end for Satan. By the death, burial, and resurrection of Jesus Christ, HE WOULD BRING MANY SONS UNTO GLORY. But first the captain of our salvation must be made perfect through suffering.

Learn this lesson from this important study—if you are a child of God, Satan hates you! Make no mistake about it. Satan goes about like a roaring lion seeking whom he may devour, but we are not ignorant of his devices. We know we shall be more than conquerors through Jesus Christ, our Lord.

CHAPTER EIGHT

THE ORGANIZATION OF ANGELS

There is a definite order in the creation. When the Lord God made man, it is stated clearly and concisely He made him lower in order than the angels. David said in Psalm 8:3-6:

"When I consider thy heavens, the work of thy fingers, the moon and the stars, which thou hast ordained; WHAT IS MAN, that thou art mindful of him? and the son of man, that thou visitest him? FOR THOU HAST MADE HIM A LITTLE LOWER THAN THE ANGELS, and hast crowned him with glory and honour. Thou madest him to have dominion over the works of thy hands; thou hast put all things under his feet."

Notice carefully these words: "Thou hast made him a little lower than the angels." When God determined to make man He did not use the angels as His pattern. He said, "Let us make man in our image and AFTER OUR LIKENESS." In later chapters we will study the creation of man in detail, but here we want to deal with the angels—their creation and their organization. If you have never heard about these things, pay close attention.

Our word, "angel" comes from the Greek word, "angelos"

meaning, literally, "messenger." In this way we could better understand its meaning. I say that because we find that there are messengers of God who are angels in the heavenly sense, and there are messengers of God who are ministers of the Gospel right here on earth.

For example, take the account of Acts 27. The Apostle Paul was on board ship bound for Rome when a terrible storm arose. When the storm was at its height, Paul called the crew of the ship together and said to them,

> "Sirs, ye should have hearkened unto me, and not have loosed from Crete, and to have gained this harm and loss. And now I exhort you to be of good cheer: for there shall be no loss of any man's life among you, but of the ship. For there stood by me this night THE ANGEL OF GOD, whose I am, and whom I serve, saying, Fear not, Paul; thou must be brought before Caesar: and lo, God hath given thee all them that sail with thee."
>
> (Acts 27:21–24)

This messenger, with a message from God, was an angel of the heavenly rank.

In the Book of Revelation we see "angels" who are messengers of God but who are men who have been called of God into divine service. We read Christ

> "had in his right hand seven stars: and out of his mouth went a sharp two-edged sword: and his countenance was as the sun shineth in his strength . . . The seven stars are the ANGELS of the seven churches."
>
> (Rev. 1:16,20)

This does not mean the seven churches of Asia had angelic heavenly beings overshadowing them. It means the pastors of the seven churches were true "messengers" of God who were being held in the right hand of Christ.

HEAVENLY MESSENGERS

It is my purpose in this chapter to deal with the "heavenly" messengers, the angels of the celestial realm. The Scriptures tell us the angels of heaven were seemingly created in ranks of graduations of power. The best way to think of them is as an army. In fact, this is the term used by the Prophet Daniel. He said,

> "And all the inhabitants of the earth are reputed as nothing: and he doeth according to his will in the ARMY of heaven, and among the inhabitants of the earth: and none can stay his hand, or say unto him, What doest thou?"
>
> (Dan. 4:35)

In the ranks of the ARMY OF HEAVEN there are at least nine grades of authority mentioned in the Bible. They are: cherubim, seraphim, archangels, mighty angels, thrones, dominions, principalities, powers, and the lesser angels. We further learn that some of each rank rebelled with Lucifer, but many more remained loyal to the Lord God of heaven and earth.

The Bible further teaches that the angels of God and the fallen angels of Satan war in the heavenlies. We, who are the redeemed of God, join them in this incredible warfare.

Let me substantiate this statement by quoting the words of the Apostle Paul in Ephesians 6:11,12.

> "Put on the whole armour of God, that ye may be able to stand against the whiles of the devil. For we wrestle not against flesh and blood, but against PRINCIPALITIES, against POWERS, against the rulers of the darkness of this world, against spiritual wickedness in high places."

The spiritual wickedness in "high places," is translated, "heavenly places," in the Revised Standard Version. The New English Bible says

> "For our fight is not against human foes, but against COSMIC POWERS, against the AUTHORITIES and POTENTATES of this dark world, against the super-human forces of EVIL IN THE HEAVENS."

These Scriptures state clearly that the warfare of the true believer is against fallen spiritual powers in the "heavenlies."

Now to the other part of the statement that the true angels of God war with the fallen angels of Satan, and this warfare is in the heavenlies.

We are told of this unseen battle in Daniel 10. This is a most intriguing chapter in the Bible. Let me give you a setting of what took place in the life of this man. Daniel had been reading the prophecy of Jeremiah and was searching it carefully. He came to a portion of the prophet's writing which he did not understand. So he prayed to God for enlightenment. He very definitely set his mind upon the matter so he could gain understanding of what Jeremiah was speaking. Daniel prayed and sought the face of God for three full weeks and heard nothing. The heavens were seemingly closed above his head. Suddenly on the twenty-first day, a man stood before him. Daniel described the man in this way.

"Then I lifted up mine eyes, and looked, and
behold a certain man clothed in linen, whose loins
were girded with fine gold of Uphaz: his body also
was like the beryl, and his face as the appearance
of lightning, and his eyes as lamps of fire, and his
arms and his feet like in colour to polished brass,
and the voice of his words like the voice of a
multitude."

(Dan. 10:5,6)

Daniel's account says when this person appeared before
him, he was not alone. The incident frightened him and his
companions.

" . . . a great quaking fell upon them, so that they
fled to hide themselves."

Reading carefully, we come to the realization that this one
who appeared to Daniel was an angel. This angel had an
amazing story to tell. He began to relate it as Daniel stood
trembling before him. The angel recounted that as soon as
Daniel had prayed (21 days before) his prayer was heard
immediately in heaven. He (the angel) had been sent with the
answer. On the way to Daniel, from the presence of God, this
angel had to pass through territory guarded by angels who
were faithful to Satan. The angels of opposition evidently
were of those called "principalities." The angel said,

"But the prince of the kingdom of Persia withstood
me one and twenty days."

(Dan. 10:13)

The angel who was sent from God with Daniel's angels
appeared upon the scene. It was none other than Michael, an

archangel. As soon as Michael joined the battle, the angel with the message for Daniel was allowed to continue on his mission. The Bible relates,

> "But, lo, Michael, one of the chief princes, came to help me."

Here Michael, the archangel, also was called one of the chief princes of the Lord God.

After the angel had given Daniel the answer to his prayer, he spoke of his own immediate plans. He said,

> "Now will I return to fight with the prince of Persia: and when I am gone forth, lo, the prince of Grecia shall come."
>
> (vs. 20)

This Bible teaching in Daniel shows clearly the various rank of authority among the angels of both the Lord and Satan. The angel dispatched with Daniel's message was of lesser rank than the principalities of Persia and Greece. These angels are spirits without mortal bodies which can be killed. So their work can only be thwarted by a greater authority and greater force to hinder them and push them back. Michael, the arch-angel, was of greater force and authority than the princes of Persia and Greece.

This is in direct accord with the teaching of Jesus when He spoke of Satan and his power as that of "a strong man." Jesus said,

> "But if I cast out devils by the Spirit of God, then the kingdom of God is come unto you. Or else how can one enter INTO A STRONG MAN'S

HOUSE and spoil his goods, EXCEPT HE FIRST
BIND THE STRONG MAN? and then he will
spoil his house."

(Mat. 12:28,29)

We have another instance depicting the ranks of the
angelic hosts in the New Testament. It is recorded in Jude 8
and 9.

"Likewise also these filthy dreamers defile the
flesh, despise DOMINION, and speak EVIL OF
DIGNITIES. Yet Michael the archangel, when
contending with the devil he disputed about the
body of Moses, durst not bring against him a
railing accusation, but said, THE LORD RE-
BUKE THEE."

The Scriptures do not state clearly when this took place,
but it might have been when Moses appeared with Jesus and
Elijah on the Mount of Transfiguration. Satan held all the
souls of the departed dead in sheol, a place for the dead,
located in the center of the earth. The souls of all the
righteous dead, including Moses, were there too, waiting for
the price of redemption to be paid. Michael was dispatched
to bring up Moses from sheol. He was withstood by Satan,
and, no doubt, Satan told him it would not be allowed.
Michael, the mighty archangel of the Lord, was not of the
same rank as fallen Lucifer, who became Satan. There was
nothing Michael could do to Satan. The Bible says Michael
"durst not" bring against him a railing accusation. The words
"durst not" mean he dared not. Why did Michael dare not
rail on the devil? Because Satan was of greater position than
he. Michael simply said, "The Lord rebuke thee," or "I refer

you to the Lord regarding this matter. It is by His authority I do this."

This matter of respect of authority is practically unknown to the average Christian. In fact, many in the church of Jesus Christ despise authority and speak evil of dignities. They do not know that in the church, the Lord Jesus has given to every man "a measure of faith." (Rom. 12:3) And with this measure of faith comes his measure of authority. Christ has put in the church apostles, prophets, evangelists, pastors, and teachers—men of authority.

From this lesson in Daniel we should learn that if the angels of God are limited in authority, and Michael the archangel could not rail against Satan, then we also are limited in our authority and should be careful we do not bite off more than we can handle.

In Mark 16 we are told believers in the Lord Jesus Christ can " ... in my name shall they cast out devils." This word "devils" should be "demons". When we cast out demons, we do not cast out Satan, personally, but only lesser messengers of authority.

The display of the forces of Satan, as recorded by Daniel, leads us to believe that the entire globe is organized under principalities, corresponding to earthly governments. If there is a Prince of Persia and a Prince of Greece, we can be assured there is a Prince of Russia, a Prince of Germany, a Prince of America, etc. These princes are the rulers of the darkness of this world. Who is behind all the killing, stealing and destroying? Satan and his hosts! This is not mere conjecture. It is bluntly stated in the Scriptures that the government of this earth is in the hands of Satan.

But those of us who have fled to the refuge, our Lord Jesus Christ, need not fear. Satan is powerful, but OUR GOD IS ALL POWERFUL. You can be sure we are protected by the unseen hosts of heaven. Nothing can touch us unless it be the permissive will of the Almighty. Jesus pointed out He could pray to the Father who would immediately give Him more than 12 legions of angels. (Mt. 26:53) A "legion" in the Roman army was 6,100 men and 726 horsemen. Twelve legions would be 81,912 angels who could be dispatched to help our Lord Jesus Christ if He needed them.

In Hebrews 12:22, we are told when we come into the presence of God in prayer, we are surrounded by an "innumerable company of angels."

By the same token, remember the maniac at Godara who said his name was "legion" because he had a legion of demons within him. If we take this same word and its meaning literally, we could say he had 6,826 demons tormenting him. Is it any wonder he was a maniac?

I tell you solemnly, THE LORD JESUS CHRIST IS OUR ONLY PLACE OF SAFETY.

Though an host should encamp against us, our God is the God of Deliverance.

CHAPTER NINE

THE COURT OF HEAVEN

Our study now takes us to the account in the Bible of a great man named Job. Satan made a direct attack upon him. We shall see why and how this was done and also the final result. We are studying the ways of angels and Satan so we might be thoroughly equipped and furnished in our warfare against the hosts of Satan. We are going to be "more than conquerors through Jesus Christ our Lord."

In this lesson we see how Satan attacked a man who belonged to God. In later lessons we shall see how Satan attacks men who do not belong to the household of faith. The difference is astounding.

I do not believe the Book of Job is a parable or an allegory. I believe it to be literal history. It was written for our learning, and for an example of and reason for SOME sufferings.

Job was a citizen of Uz. He had seven sons and three daughters. The stock on his farm consisted of seven thousand sheep, three thousand camels, five hundred yoke of oxen, and five hundred she asses. He had a number of servants who took care of the animals and looked after the household. Job was well set even according to Texas standards!

After the Bible record finishes the description of Job's household, the scene of the first chapter suddenly shifts to the heavens. We read

"Let Us Make Man . . . "

> "Now there came a day when the sons of God came to present themselves before the Lord, and Satan came also among them."

This one verse says a great deal. It tells us that periodically the courts of heaven convene and all the angelic hosts of heaven are present to give an account of their activities. Even the fallen hosts and Satan are compelled to be present.

> "And the Lord said unto Satan, Whence comest thou? Then Satan answered the Lord, and said, From going to and fro IN THE EARTH, and from walking up and down in it."

This leaves little doubt as to where Satan had been and where was his interest. He had been to and fro, and up and down, IN THE EARTH. During his journeys he received reports from the various orders of his hierarchy, the principalities, powers, thrones, dominions, etc. Let me state here a fact we must thoroughly and completely understand. SATAN IS NOT OMNIPRESENT. Satan is not God. He CANNOT be everywhere at one time. If he is in California, he cannot be in Berlin. If he is in London, he cannot be in Cairo! But, he is represented everywhere ALL THE TIME by his hierarchy of demons and powers. His ambassadors are everywhere.

During Satan's travels to and fro and up and down in the earth, he was informed about a man in Uz whose name was Job. Now, this same man about whom he had heard, also was brought to his attention by the Almighty.

> "And the Lord said unto Satan, Hast thou considered my servant Job, that there is none like him IN

THE EARTH, a perfect and an upright man, one that feareth God, and escheweth evil?"

Notice, please, the Eternal called Job, MY SERVANT. The Lord God was proud of Job and of his integrity. But when the Lord mentioned Job to Satan, it brought an instant verbal response.

> "Then Satan answered the Lord, and said, Doth Job fear God for nought? Hast not thou made AN HEDGE ABOUT HIM, and about his house, and about all that he hath on every side? thou hast blessed the work of his hands, and his substance is increased in the land."
>
> (v. 9,10)

Here Satan mentioned one of the most glorious truths contained in the entire Bible. GOD HAD A HEDGE AROUND JOB WHICH NEITHER SATAN NOR HIS DEMONS COULD PENETRATE. If this isn't security and safety, then I would like to know what is!

This statement made by Satan is very revealing. How did Satan know there was a hedge about Job? I am sure he knew this by experience. No doubt, he had tried to attack Job's person, his family, his finances, and the work of his hands. No doubt, Satan had tried every conceivable angle and device to gain any advantage over Job but all to no avail. Satan ran into the hedge every time! In admitting there was a hedge around Job, Satan admitted he had tried to reach Job but without success. Satan thought if he could penetrate that hedge, things would be different. However, he openly admitted he could not get through the hedge.

What was this inpenetrable hedge? We know it was not a

tangible hedge as we would have around a yard—a privet hedge or a hedge of roses. No doubt, the hedge was made up of angels! David said,

> "The angel of the Lord encampeth (hedges) round about them that fear him, and delivereth them."
>
> (Psa. 34:7)

Jesus said,

> "Take heed that ye despise not one of these little ones; for I say unto you, That in heaven THEIR ANGELS DO ALWAYS behold the face of my Father which is in heaven."
>
> (Mt. 18:10)

In Hebrews 1:14, we are told that the angels

> "are all ministering spirits, SENT FORTH TO MINISTER for them who shall be HEIRS OF SALVATION."

Angels know the limit set for Satan.

When the Lord God builds a hedge about His own, no one can penetrate it. It is our defense and Satan's obstacle. He would strike us if he could. His arm is long enough, but God intervenes. THANK GOD FOR THE HEDGE!

Satan made an accusation.

> "But put forth thine hand now, and touch all that he hath, and he will curse thee to thy face."
>
> (v.11)

90

Satan is saying, "Take down your hedge, let me touch him, and you will see how upright and fine Job really is. He serves you for what he receives from you. Withhold from him. Take it all away, and he will curse you to your face."

The Lord agreed to take down the hedge but with a definite limitation. Satan was given permission to do what he pleased with the family and possessions of Job, but he was forbidden to touch the person of Job. So Satan went from the presence of God to attack Job.

SATAN'S LIMITED POWER

This account of Job makes it very clear that the power of Satan is limited. He can do only what God allows him to do. We who are the children of God need have no fear of Satan for he is allowed to work on us only under the surveillance of the Almighty. God's eyes are always upon His own. He knows if we are strong enough to bear it.

Satan went into action against the family of Job and his possessions. While his children were eating, their house fell and killed them all. His servants were murdered. His goods were stolen. The fortunes of Job were brought to a total collapse.

One point of this account of the attacks of Satan against the house and possessions of Job fascinates me. It is the fact of Satan's power to disturb the weather and use it for his ends. The account reads:

"And behold, there came a great wind from the wilderness, and smote the four corners of the house, and it fell upon the young men, and they are dead."

The question arises, "Can Satan move the elements by the permissive will of God?" The answer is a definite, "Yes!"

I am sure you are familiar with the account of Jesus in a boat with His disciples when, suddenly, a great storm arose. Jesus was asleep in the boat. The disciples, though all were seasoned fishermen, were frightened by the intensity of the storm. They awoke Jesus and said, "Don't you care that we perish?" Jesus, with calm assurance, raised His voice against the winds and said, "Peace, be still." Immediately, there was a great calm. Jesus was not simply showing off by changing the course of the winds and weather. It seems this storm had been directed by Satan in an effort to kill the Son of God before He could go to the cross. Jesus rebuked the winds, not for disturbing his sleep, but because they were winds of destruction.

When Satan finished his work of destruction against Job, he sat back hoping to witness a man questioning and accusing God for deserting him. But, instead, though Job's emotions were wounded and he mourned for his children, Satan heard Job say,

> "Naked came I out of my mother's womb, and naked shall I return thither; the Lord gave, and the Lord hath taken away; blessed be the name of the Lord."
>
> (v. 20,21)

Then Job arose, rent his mantle, shaved his head as a sign of mourning, fell upon the ground, and WORSHIPPED GOD! (How and when do you worship God?)

The next time the courts of heaven convened, Satan came with his report. The Lord God said to Satan,

"Hast thou considered my servant Job? Still he holdeth fast his integrity, although thou movedst me against him, to destroy him without cause."

(2:3)

With a snarl, Satan retorted,

"Skin for skin, yea, all that a man hath will he give for his life. But put forth thine hand now, and touch his bone and his flesh, and he will curse thee to thy face.

"And the Lord said unto Satan, Behold, he is in thine hand; BUT SAVE HIS LIFE."

Now Satan had permission to actually touch Job though not to the point of death. Here, again, we see some of the power possessed by Satan. He has the power to bring disease and suffering upon man, and, where he is permitted, even death. So,

"Satan smote Job with sore boils from the sole of his foot unto his crown."

SICKNESS AND SATAN

There is little doubt in the minds of thinking people that Satan can afflict. But, often I am asked whether or not Satan can heal. I will endeavor to be concise on this point.

First, SATAN CANNOT HEAL; HE IS ABLE ONLY TO LIFT THE AFFLICTION TO DECEIVE. This he can do through those who belong to him who are not the children of God. The Bible says in 2 Timothy 2:25,26:

"In meekness instructing those that oppose themselves; if God peradventure will give them repentance to the acknowledging of the truth; and that
they may recover themselves out of the SNARE
OF THE DEVIL, WHO ARE TAKEN CAPTIVE
BY HIM AT HIS WILL."

Here we are told about those who are taken captive by the
devil at any time he so desires whom he then uses to deceive.
He afflicts and then lifts the affliction, in an effort to bring
confusion to the real work of God which brings healing to
the sick and afflicted. This certainly describes the false
Christs mentioned in the Bible who work lying wonders and
miracles. These are those who professed to do mighty
miracles in His name and to whom He said, "Depart from
me, ye workers of iniquity. I never knew you." Satan
attempts to counterfeit every true purpose of God. He does
this to DECEIVE. And deception is one of his mightiest
tools.

Job suffered great mental anguish at the death of his
children and the loss of his possessions. But now he was
suffering physical pain that was almost unbearable. At this
point, Satan attacked Job with something even worse than
the boils—his wife turned against him. She failed completely
to comprehend what was happening to her husband. She
became A TOOL OF SATAN!

This can happen very easily if we do not learn how to
guard our tongues. She said, "Dost thou still retain thine
integrity? Curse God and die." Job's reply came from a heart
of courage.

"Thou speakest as one of the foolish women

speaketh. What? shall we receive good at the hand
of God, and shall we not receive evil?

In other words, "Did God ever promise us a bed of roses?
Were we ever told we would have no problems or troubles?
We never were told we would be immune from the trials of
life. God can do with us as He sees fit."

What is the end of the story? Job endured! The testing
ended. God healed Job. All he lost was doubly restored.
History learned the devil was a liar. The world learned there
are some men who love God because He is God and for no
other reason.

Generations have learned, though Satan is a powerful foe
who can afflict and, if permitted, can take a life, he can do
nothing against the Christian unless it is the permissive will
of God. We have learned, if we who are the sons of God in
the midst of a wicked and perverse generation will maintain
our integrity, we are more than conquerors through Jesus
Christ our Lord. This means we will have troubles and
skirmishes with the enemy but we will come out of them as
overcomers. And we always have something left over. There
are always spoils from the battle. We are MORE than
conquerors—conquerors who come out of trouble with no
losses on their books, only profits and with all resources
intact!

"Behold, we count them happy which endure. Ye
have heard of the patience of Job, and have seen
the end of the Lord; that the Lord is very pitiful,
and of tender mercy."

(James 5:11)

The next time the courts of heaven convened, Satan's mouth was full of dust. But you can be sure when Satan went away licking his wounds, he vowed there would be another day!

Have you ever considered the fact that God and Satan might be talking about you the next time the courts of heaven convene? What will be the results of your testing?

CHAPTER TEN

KNOWING OUR ENEMY

In 2 Corinthians 2:10,11, we read these words:

> "To whom ye forgive anything, I forgive also: for
> if I forgave anything, to whom I forgave it, for
> your sakes forgave I it in the person of Christ: Lest
> SATAN should get an advantage of us: FOR WE
> ARE NOT IGNORANT OF HIS DEVICES."

A device is an arrangement, plan, scheme, project, contrivance, plot, strategy, or trick. A device is the work of the mind. In other words, Satan has plans, tricks, schemes, and plots, to trip us and spoil the purpose of God in our individual lives. He endeavors to overtake us at a disadvantage, but the Apostle Paul said he was not ignorant of Satan's devices. Paul, through experience, had learned the devices of Satan, or, better said, he had learned Satan's method of operation.

This is very important to those of us who name the Name of Christ. We must become acquainted with the way Satan's mind works.

In Ephesians 6:11, we are told:

> "Put on the whole armour of God, that ye may be
> able to stand against the WILES OF THE
> DEVIL."

This word "wiles" is practically synonymous with the word, "devices." Another word similar in meaning is "methods". Putting together the ideas expressed by these words, we find the Scripture tells us the Christian should know the workings of Satan's mind against him. But it is apparent we do not have many informed Christians in spite of the fact that we have thousands and thousands of churches. My purpose in this book is to convey Bible teaching and information.

The primary work of Satan is to "blind our minds," and keep us in the dark concerning vital truths. In 2 Corinthians 4:4 we are told:

> "In whom the god of this world (Satan) hath blinded the MINDS of them which believe not, lest the light of the glorious gospel of Christ, who is the image of God, should shine unto them."

Think of it! Satan's chief desire is to blind the mind. His strategy is to keep us from giving thought and consideration to matters which are vital to our lives.

BLINDED TOWARD SATAN

One of the areas where Satan uses every device to blind is the area of his personal existence. If he can deceive a man into thinking he does not exist, that the idea of a devil is a lot of superstitious nonsense, he has blinded that mind in a very vulnerable area. To deny the existence of Satan leads to the denial of God's Word, which, ultimately, leads to the denial of God Himself. And, if there is no God, there is no pardon from sin, no help beyond the human, and man is left to his own helplessness.

This is how Satan's mind works. If he can deceive you into thinking you have no enemy, you will not prepare a defense. Why put on the armour of God if there is no one to fight? Then when he attacks, we have no defense and are overcome easily.

Once we begin to tamper with God's Word, there is no end to deception. If there is no personal Satan, then there is no personal God who said there is a personal devil and enemy. If there is no heaven, there is no hell. If there is no sin and no author of sin, then there is no eternal judge who shall one day judge all sin. If the Bible is not truth, then there is no lie or father of lies.

One of the great truths which proves the devil exists, acts, and succeeds, is the fact that he has the intelligent world believing he is not real.

Many have laid aside the belief in the personal existence of Satan because of all the silly superstitious nonsense that has been propogated about him. Satan DOES NOT have a RED SUIT, horns on his head, a forked tail, and a pitch-fork in his hand.

This idea developed in the middle ages when stage plays were presented in cities and villages. They had a casting problem. A costume was needed for the one who took the part of the devil, a costume which the audience would recognize as the devil. Someone came up with the idea of a red suit, horns on the head, cloven hoofs, and a forked tail. Furthermore, many false ideas were presented in these plays which have almost become accepted as theological facts but which are totally without Scriptural foundation.

For instance, the devil has been protrayed a thousand times as the keeper of hell whose main occupation is to keep the fires of hell from going out. The Scriptural facts are the devil is NOT NOW in hell, NEVER HAS BEEN IN HELL, and does not know what hell is apart from the Word of God. The Bible DOES teach a day is coming when Satan shall be cast into hell, PREPARED BY GOD FOR THE DEVIL AND HIS ANGELS. He will be there as a prisoner, not as a ruler, caretaker, jailer, and tormenter.

Nothing could be further from the truth than to speak of "Satan's hell." SATAN HAS NO HELL. There is only one hell—God's hell. God prepared it. What could be plainer than the words of Matthew 25:41: "Then shall He (Christ) say unto them on the left hand, Depart from me, ye cursed, into everlasting fire, PREPARED FOR THE DEVIL AND HIS ANGELS."

The Lord Jesus taught very definitely it is our God who has the power of eternal punishment and who exercises it. Jesus said, "Fear not them which kill the body, and which are not able to kill the soul; but rather fear him (God) who is able to destroy both soul and body in hell." (Mt. 10:28)

The devil certainly knows all the Bible says about him and he understands it very well. The Bible says the demons also believe and tremble. (Jsd. 2:19) But in their believing they do not submit their wills to the will of God. In spite of their believing, they are at war with the Almighty just like many people.

Satan is very real. Don't be fooled on this matter!

Now, another truth we must understand is that at Calvary, Satan was exposed to the gaze of the hosts of heaven. They know it is just a matter of time until Christ shall execute the sentence of judgment already passed against Satan. The hosts of heaven know this too, but Satan is endeavoring to keep each generation blinded to this fact. One of Satan's favorite devices is to make you think he has more power than he really has, and that his power is independent of God's power and not subject to it. In our study of Job we saw Satan could do nothing against this servant of God unless the Eternal allowed it. Satan was subject to God. And Satan doesn't like it so he lies about it.

Satan has power, but he does not have ALL power. Jesus said of Himself, after His death, burial, and resurrection,

> "ALL power is given UNTO ME in heaven and in earth."
>
> (Mt. 28:18)

Satan is a created creature—he is not the creator.

The Apostle John taught the church,

> "Greater is he that is in you than he that is in the World."
>
> (1 John 4:4)

We sing this truth in our services in Bethesda. A constant means of teaching truth to ourselves is by Psalms, hymns, and spiritual songs. The song goes this way:

"Greater is He that is within you,

Than he that is in the world.

Greater is He that is within you,

Than he that is in the world.

Greater than angels or powers;

Greater than this life or death.

Greater is He, greater is He,

Greater is Christ our Lord!"

You, as a believer, have Christ within you WHO IS GREATER THAN SATAN.

SATAN NOT OMNIPRESENT

A common error that has crept in to the church is that Satan is omnipresent (present everywhere at the same time). Satan cannot be present in Chicago and London at the same time. He cannot be in Africa and San Francisco at the same time. He is a creature, limited in time and space.

Another truth to constantly keep in mind is that not very many people ever have a personal encounter with Satan in their lifetime. Many of the great men of the Bible never had an open encounter with Satan. Elisha never met a personal attack of Satan. Neither did Daniel. Of the Apostle Paul we read, "a messenger of Satan was sent to buffet him." This was by the express permission of God to keep Paul humble. Because of the abundance of revelations given to Paul, it would have been very easy for him to get puffed-up and full of pride. (2 Cor. 12)

Those who did have an encounter with Satan were: Eve, Peter, Job, Ananias, Judas Iscariot, and a few others. I say this to make clear the fact that many people are attacked by Satan's demons, not by Satan himself. This is important to know that we might realize the realm of our authority. When we are told the believer can cast out demons, it does not mean he casts out the devil. THERE IS A DIFFERENCE.

SATAN NOT OMNISCIENT

The next truth we must know is that Satan is not omniscient (having all knowledge). There is much he does not know. Satan does not know your thoughts or does he know the plan of God for your life! The Bible says if Satan had known the wisdom of God, he never would have crucified the Lord of Glory. (1 Cor. 2:8)

Satan does not know your future and cannot foretell it! For centuries Satan has deceived men into thinking they can foretell the future. History reveals there have always been sorcerers, enchanters, diviners, and star-gazers, who endeavor to make inanimate matter tell the future.

People who rely on horoscopes are deluded people. To think that sensible people would go to a drug store, buy a horoscope book and put some credence in it, is beyond my belief. To think that the stars, an inanimate creation, have power to decide your destiny is incredible. God is against this.

Israel got into trouble with God when they built high places or towers and made them towers of the Zodiac. They made up signs of the Zodiac which means: "Men with animal bodies," and delved into matters which were none of their business.

Don't follow ocult religion. This is demon worship. The way of Christ is the only way; the only safe way. Jesus said,

"I am the way, the truth, and the life, NO MAN cometh to the Father BUT BY ME."

WE ARE NOT IGNORANT OF SATAN'S DEVICES!

CHAPTER ELEVEN

RUNNING BEFORE OUR TIME

Our theme study verse is found in 2 Corinthians 2:11: "Lest Satan should get an advantage of us: for we are not ignorant of his devices." Literally, this means "we are not ignorant of the way that Satan's mind works."

Satan wants to blind our minds through lies because he is the "Father of lies." Here are some of the lies:

1. He lies about his existence. He uses devices to blind us in the area of his personal existence. If he can convince you there is no devil, he has won a great victory.

2. He lies about the extent of his power.

3. He lies with the impression he dwells everywhere and can attack at will, when it is only the work of his demons which can be resisted and cast out by every TRUE BELIEVER IN CHRIST.

4. He lies about his knowledge, deceiving people to believe their destiny is written in the stars. They become deluded sorcerers, enchanters, diviners, etc.

SATAN IS A LIAR!

A very cunning device of Satan which I want to discuss in this lesson is: The device of causing us to hurry and run before our time. If we are not careful, we will find ourselves endeavoring to get God to say "Yes," to our schemes and plans and fail to wait for the leaderhip of God.

The underlying theme of all of these messages is THE MANIFESTATION OF THE SONS OF GOD. It is the desire of God to manifest Himself through His children whom He calls HIS SONS. We never will be used as sons of God unless we grow and mature in the things pertaining to the Kingdom of God. This is my reason for these lessons: To teach you what sonship is and how to take your position as "the sons of God in the midst of a crooked and perverse generation."

Again we must settle the fact that without the leadership of God, there is no sonship. Romans 8:14, tells us:

> "For as many as are led by the Spirit of God, they are the sons of God."

WE DON'T LEAD GOD; HE LEADS US.

The Christian life is not an endeavor to get God to do our will, it is a life of submitting ourselves to the will and purpose of God. This something Satan never wanted to do. He does not want to do the will of God, and he will entice whoever he can away from the will of God by every conceivable means. Again I repeat, one of his most subtle devices is to cause us to become impatient and run before our time.

THE TEMPTATIONS OF JESUS

This device was used by Satan in the temptations of Jesus. When Jesus Christ came into the world it is said of Him: "Lo, I come to do THY WILL, O God." (Heb. 10:7) The will of God was His delight. So Satan began to tempt Jesus on the premise that the will of God was the long way of doing things. It insinuated, "Don't wait for God. Use your own initiative. After all, you need not be utterly dependent upon the Father."

As we turn to Luke 4, we see where Jesus Christ the Son of God began His ministry among men. As we examine His beginnings carefully, we learn invaluable lessons for "He was tempted of the devil. And in those days he did eat nothing: And when they were ended, he afterward hungered. And the devil said unto him, If thou be the Son of God, command this stone that it be made bread."

The Bible account says:

> "And Jesus being full of the Holy Ghost returned from Jordan, and was led by the Spirit into the wilderness, being forty days tempted of the devil. And in those days he did eat nothing: and when they were ended, he afterward hungered. And the devil said unto him, If thou be the Son of God, command this stone that it be made bread."

Here was the first temptation of the devil to cause Jesus Christ to live independently of the leadership of the Father. He said, "Don't just stand there! Do something! If you are the Son of God, prove it. What are you waiting for?" Jesus was waiting for direction from the Almighty! Jesus' answer to Satan was: "It is written, That man shall not live by bread alone, but be every word of God."

Every man who names the name of Christ must learn to wait for the Word of God for leadership and direction. Do not allow yourself to be rushed by the sly devices of Satan. More people have been ruined for the kingdom of God by running before their time than any other way. They see needs and problems in the world. They see people milling around without spiritual leadership. So they get the mistaken idea that the need constitutes a calling, and they just must do something about it. They must change the world!

No one knew the world needed changing, any more than Jesus. But He also knew He had to wait until He was made perfect through sufferings. He knew He had to go to the cross in God's perfect time.

We, who are the children of God, must learn to discipline our desire to change the world before we ourselves are changed. DON'T ALLOW SATAN TO RUSH YOU INTO PREMATURE ACTIVITY.

Jesus had to suppress his desire for bread when He was hungry and wait for the leadership of God. He disciplined Himself to remain in right and perfect relationship to the Father.

The disciples of Jesus didn't fall into the snare of beginning with others—they started with themselves. THEY WOULD NOT allow themselves to be rushed. They didn't start by trying to change the world—they started by changing themselves. If they had begun by attempting to change the world, they would have been meddlers. But because they began with themselves, they became MESSENGERS.

The wait for ten days in the City of Jerusalem for the coming of the Holy Spirit baptism was one of the wisest moves in history. During ten days, the men who were to change the world were changed and made witnesses instead of moralists. They told what had happened to them. Those who heard them, wanted what they saw and heard.

Jesus emphasized this place of beginning when He said:

"Why do you see the speck that is in your brother's eye, but do not notice the log that is in your own eye? You hypocrite, first take the log out of your own eye, and then you will see clearly to take the speck out of your brother's eye."

(Mt. 7:3,5)

108

Begin with yourself. Then you will see clearly to help others. Don't allow Satan to hurry you!

Nothing is more pathetic than to see people who have inner problems and conflicts trying to work toward world peace. When I see pictures in the papers of a hippie crowd demonstrating for world peace, I marvel. How can these people expect to handle world problems when they cannot handle their own personal problems? They have never learned to wash the dirt from the world. They are starting in the wrong place. They are in a mistaken hurry. They have missed the most important first step.

Another sad picture is to see people who have no inner integration trying to integrate others. They are cases dealing with cases.

The other day I noticed in one of the advice columns of a newspaper that the wife of a psychiatrist was inquiring about the problems her husband was having. Here was a man who was full of conflicts trying to solve the conflicts of others. This is tragic.

The disciples took hold of the right end of the stick. They took hold of themselves first. They would not allow Satan to push them out prematurely.

Remember the question Peter asked Jesus, "Jesus, what about this man, John?" The reply was, "What is that to you? Follow me!" Peter was wrong in concerning himself first with what the other man was going to do. He should have been primarily concerned with himself.

SECOND TEMPTATION

The second temptation of Jesus was this:

"And the devil, taking him up into an high mountain, shewed him all the kingdoms of the world in

a moment of time. And the devil said unto him, All
this power will I give thee, and the glory of them:
for that is delivered unto me; and to whomsoever
I will I give it. If thou therefore wilt worship me,
all shall be thine."

(Lk. 4:5–7)

Here was the same insidious device of Satan—the device
of the SHORT CUT. "Don't take God's way to glory and
authority. It takes too long. After all, we are in a hurry. Do
it my way."

I have seen short-cuts ruin many good people. They very
plainly allowed Satan to push them out before their time.
They thought they were ready to evangelize the world, and
pastor a church. Later they found out, much to their chagrin,
they had run prematurely.

I often think of Jesus Christ, the Son of God, who was shut
up unto God for thirty years. He waited until it was God's
time to use him. When that time came, He was ready and
available. Thirty years seems like such a long period of
enforced idleness. But, in reality, it was not at all idleness. He
was learning the ways of the Almighty all through these
years.

Some people will never do anything in the local church
because they feel they know everything and need to learn
nothing. So they just sit and chafe, growing bitter and
resentful, because they are not setting the world on fire for
God. They are idle and will remain idle until they learn that
faithfulness in the little things, while we are waiting for the
big things, is a law of the kingdom. Jesus said, "If you will
not be faithful in the little things, who will entrust the greater
things into your keeping?"

Think of the Apostle Paul when he was in prison. Satan

could have whipped him into terrible condemnation over sitting there in forced idleness when he could have been winning the world for Christ. But Paul said,

> "I want you to know, brethren, that what has happened to me has really served to advance the gospel."
>
> (Phil. 1:12)

His imprisonment advanced the Gospel far beyond his immediate conception. He said,

> "Most of the brethren have been made confident in the Lord because of my imprisonment, and are much more bold to speak the word of God without fear."
>
> (vs. 14)

But a far greater result than inspiring the brethren to preach more boldly came out of his imprisonment—his writings—his epistles. They have touched generations for ages and still mold our thoughts and actions.

Paul might have chafed at the seeming lack of providence on the part of God—a providence which allowed injustice to prevail and to keep him locked behind bars. He was shut off from his beloved preaching. But one of the best things that ever happened to Paul was when he was restrained from preaching. It set him to writing. His preaching might have died with him, but his epistles live on.

Paul, at times, seemed to have been enticed by the enemy to rush ahead. In the account of the Book of Acts we read that he was ready to lead his evangelistic party into Asia when the Holy Spirit said, "No." So they headed for Bithynia. Again they were forbidden by God. Why? The Lord had something better—THE WILL OF GOD.

Paul had a vision in which he saw a man from Macedonia saying, "Come over into Macedonia and help us." Because Paul was led by God and didn't just run at his own discretion, he was used to open the door to the continent of Europe with the message of the saving grace of Jesus Christ.

Jesus would not allow Himself to be pushed by Satan to take short-cuts. Be wise enough to learn this same lesson carefully.

Perhaps you are one who has been trying for a long time to get God to say, "Yes," to your plans and wishes. You are finding out He will not do it. Settle down. Stop running. Tell Satan to get behind you. WAIT FOR THE DIRECTION OF GOD.

CHAPTER TWELVE

CAPTIVATED MINDS

A device is a scheme of the mind. It is an arrangement, plan, project, contrivance, plot, strategy or trick. When the Apostle Paul says, "we are not ignorant of (Satan's) devices," he is saying we are not ignorant of the WAY SATAN'S MIND WORKS.

In this lesson, we study more tricks used by Satan in his work against us to keep us blinded and inwardly unchanged.

I want to make a very clear, precise, deliberate statement to which I trust you will give due consideration.

Satan cannot possess the true believer in Christ. But he does war against our minds to harass, confuse, and oppress us!

Because of this war against our minds, many uninformed Christians have been taken captive. They have lost their joy and zest for living, and have become bitter, resentful, critical people. This should not be so.

Jesus spoke of salt which had lost its savor. Many live in a savorless state, a state without taste. This happened because they allowed themselves to become disappointed with life. They expected to get more out of life than they received. Now they nurse a grudge against the world. They harbor a festering sore of resentment.

I am afraid there are Christians who actually war with God in their minds because they think they didn't receive from Christianity what they felt they should. Some become angry with God because He didn't make them rich, healthy, or prominent. THIS IS WRONG. We do not serve God for reward. We love God for Himself. We cannot expect payment for loving others. Peter said to Jesus, "Lo, we have left all to follow you. Now, what do we get out of it?" Peter was looking for a reward, something added to what he already had. He had Jesus; what more did he want? Peter did not understand.

Do not allow Satan to start a war in your mind against God. Don't feel sorry for yourself because you think you have been mistreated. The ranks of Christianity are honeycombed with people who are steeped in self-pity, who sit around feeling sorry for themselves.

Inner unhappiness and inner conflicts are the chief causes of confusion in the world. When we project our inner unhappiness upon our surroundings, we disrupt them. If you cannot get along with God, you cannot get along with yourself. If you cannot get along with yourself, you cannot get along with anybody else. Sonship is getting along with God and enjoying it. The will of God is a delight, not a drudge. Don't resent God! Don't resent what He has allowed to come into your life! IT HAS COME TO CHANGE AND MOLD YOU!

Don't resent people. Extinguish the inner fires of resentment by taking all your wars to God. Empty yourself of them at the throne of confession. Allow the rain of God's presence to refresh you and bring you life. Don't allow Satan to take advantage of you through resentment.

Don't live by the attitude of the law. The prevailing attitude in the ancient world was "tit for tat"—you do this, and I do that—an eye for an eye and a tooth for a tooth. This is life on the legal "I'll pay you back" level.

Such a spirit of revenge was seen when the disciples asked

Jesus if they should call down fire from heaven on the Samaritan village which had refused to allow them to enter "because his face was set toward Jerusalem." That was race prejudice, pure and simple. But the disciples also were wrong. They tried to soften their retaliation by giving it a religious flavor, by saying the fire would come from heaven, therefore indicating divine sanction. They even claimed to have a precedent for asking this. They said, "Elijah did it."

Before the days of the Old Testament, revenge was unlimited. If a man had an eye knocked out, he had a right to knock out two others, if he could. With the coming of the Old Testament, revenge was limited to an equal measure—an eye for an eye and a tooth for a tooth. But Jesus entirely abolished revenge. Evil was to be overcome with good. The right for revenge was voided.

Yet Satan uses his wiles to keep the fires of revenge burning. How can the desire for revenge be overcome? Resist Satan—he will flee from you! And the way to resist is to FORGIVE. Forgive and forget! If you have been treated unfairly—FORGIVE. Once we start practicing revenge, there is no stopping place. It will destroy us.

I think of the disciples when Jesus said to them:

> "Behold, I send you out as lambs in the midst of wolves."
>
> (Lk. 10:3)

Of all the helpless pictures, this is the most helpless and hopeless—lambs in the midst of wolves. Naturally speaking, lambs haven't a "ghost of a chance" to survive among wolves. If they were full grown sheep, at least they could run away! In this dog-eat-dog world, lambs would be taken advantage of. This didn't seem fair.

But, Jesus' disciples were to be given a superior force on

115

the inside. Because of this, they could stop the fires of resentment and revenge. It would not be fanned any further. Resentment and revenge would stop with them.

Had the disciples allowed resentment to invade them when people mistreated them, or when they thought that God was unfair, it would have blocked and cancelled all that grace had planned. Paul, the apostle, was misunderstood and misrepresented, battered, and badgered. But he did not allow self-pity and resentment to invade him for they would have cancelled out God's work of grace in Him. He said, "I do not frustrate the grace of God" (by living under the legal concepts of the law). (Gal. 2:21) Paul did not void the grace of God by wrong attitudes. Many do. But not Paul.

In the early years of my ministry, I confess I made some serious mistakes. I retaliated at a few people who were misrepresenting things, because I resented what they were saying and doing. But, as I look back, I see I only made bad matters worse by striking back. Nothing was accomplished through my revenge. The only thing I did was give Satan an advantage which was a bad mistake. I have since learned to take matters of this kind to God in prayer. Commit them to Him. Resist Satan's device of retaliation. Stand, praying and forgiving. You will sleep better, and it puts marrow in your bones.

If you find yourself in the throes of resentment today— DON'T FIGHT. That only brings your opponent into the focus of attentions, and whatever is in the focus of attention, becomes power. Whatever arrests your attention holds you! But, whatever you do, don't suppress resentment or try to hide it. That only causes it to work in the subconscious and it will make you sick. It has been said, suppressing resentment is like canning spoiled fruit—IT WILL EXPLODE IN YOU.

Someone has defined a resentment or grudge as the "taking of stinging thorns into your bare chest, hoping that this will make the other fellow scratch." It does not work! You only punish yourself. Your resentment will not punish the other fellow.

When Jesus met Paul on the Damascus road He did not treat him as an enemy. Jesus did not try to conquer Paul with threats of punishment. He said, "Saul, why do you persecute me?" Notice in these words there is no threat of retaliation or punishment. That simple question broke down Paul's resistance. He replied, "Who are you, Lord, that I persecute you?" Suddenly Paul knew this One who stopped him and who did it without revenge, had to be the Lord!

Because of his experience with the Lord who did not practice revenge upon him, Paul later said,

> "Dearly beloved, avenge not your selves, but rather give place unto wrath: for it is written, Vengeance is mine; I will repay, saith the Lord.

> "Therefore if thine enemy hunger, feed him; if he thirst, give him drink; for in so doing thou shalt heap coals of fire on his head.

> "Be not overcome of evil, but overcome evil with good."
>
> (Rom. 12:19–21)

These are God's instructions for us. Follow them explicitly. Resist the advance of Satan against your mind. In prayer, empty out all resentment and desire for revenge. This is why many people are ill. Resentment and revenge are open doors where Satan comes in with his evil.

Satan cannot attack a man's body with infirmity unless it is by the permission of God. So he tries to enter in another way. He will work on the mind. He will endeavor to get a man worked up in his mind so he can pass the sickness of the mind to the rest of the body.

You see, the inner structure of your life was made for good will, not for ill will. The moment ill will is formed in the emotions, the color of the stomach changes, the gastric juices stop and digestion becomes disturbed. When you say, "He makes me sick," that is a fact. By your reaction of resentment against a person, the process of digestion is upset. You actually do become sick—literally sick.

Again, when you say, "He gives me a pain in the neck," that also is literally true. A tension is developed in the neck, and a pain results.

When you say, "he certainly is a headache," that is true. By your reactions to the person involved, your head begins to ache with resentments.

On the other hand, when you say, "That one is a tonic," it means you react favorably to that person with appreciation and love. Hence that person actually is a tonic. Your whole being responds and is toned up by the good will gendered. Resentments and ill feelings are contrary to the structure of God's creation, and frustration and instability is the result.

Recently I talked with a young lady who had lost her appetite, was losing weight, and felt sick all over, yet could not put her finger on any definite physical illness. She had an opportunity to visit an aunt in another state so she went. During her visit, her appetite returned and with it her health and zest for life. She began to realize her problem hinged upon her parents at home. They were always quarrelling. She resented their attitudes deeply. And this resentment was ruining her health and her entire outlook on life. She even resented going home at night. She resented her lack of happiness. But, thank God, she discovered the source of trouble in time—resentment! What did she do? She came to God in deep confession. She poured out her soul to God. He heard her and forgave her. Today, the home situation has not changed, she still lives in the same house with the same confusion, but there is no resentment in her. She does not resent her parents; now she prays for them! She learned a great lesson, one some people never learn.

Many people are not as wise as this young lady. They chew on a bitter resentment for years which eventually poisons their whole lives. Then Satan takes occasion by the whole situation to poison others. People who harbor resentments become ugly people with ugly dispositions. There is a penalty they must pay—the penalty of living with their own ugly selves for the rest of their lives. They are their own pay-off. They become lonely, forgotten people. When this happens, their adversary, the devil, sits back and laughs. His method has succeeded. He has won a victory. But, how easily all this could have been avoided. How easily he could have been defeated if that person had only known!

I must make one thing clear here. Many people are healed when they confess and rid themselves of their deep-seated resentments. But it is also true, some allow matters to continue too long and their inner life and inner organs are destroyed by the long years of stress and turmoil. Some find physical healing; some never do. But all can find mental and spiritual healing of the inner man. THIS IS THE PART OF US WHICH IS ETERNALLY IMPORTANT!

As I close this message I would leave this thought with you.

BURY YOUR RESENTMENT OR IT WILL BURY YOU. BURY IT WITH GOD IN CONFESSION, ASKING FOR FORGIVENESS. THIS COULD WELL BE YOUR DAY OF SALVATION.

CHAPTER THIRTEEN

ATTACKS AGAINST THE SOUL

It is my purpose to reveal how our enemy, or adversary, Satan ("Satan" means enemy or adversary), attacks us, who are Christians, with many and varied devices. Man is a three-part being, or what may be called a "tri-unity," meaning "a unity of three." God is a "tri-unity" of Father, Son and Holy Spirit; man is a "tri-unity" of body, soul, and spirit. Because man is a threefold being, he can expect Satan to attack him in each of these three realms: body, soul, and spirit. In this chapter I want to deal with the attacks of Satan against the soul.

First, let me clarify the use of the words body, soul, and spirit.

When God created Adam the Bible states:

> "And the Lord God formed man of the dust of the ground, and breathed into his nostrils the breath of life; and man became a LIVING SOUL."
>
> (Gen. 2:7)

This verse reveals that the BODY was made of the dust of the ground, the SPIRIT came from the breath of God, and this combination produced the SOUL. It is correct for me to say of myself, "I am a SOUL; I have a BODY; I have a SPIRIT." If we said this any other way, it just would not be

121

right nor would it sound right. I cannot say that I am a spirit with a body and a soul, because I am a mortal being. Nor can I say I am a body with a soul and spirit, for I know that I am more than a body—I am a person; I am a personality. So again I return to our original statement: I AM A SOUL, WITH A BODY AND A SPIRIT. The soul, is the self, the ego, the I.

There is little doubt in our minds that Satan can attack the body with infirmity and affliction. The Bible is filled with accounts of people who were sick, infirmed, and afflicted because of the attacks of Satan. But, we do not hear too much about his devices against the soul and spirit.

The soul is the center of the senses. Man has five senses: seeing, hearing, smelling, tasting, and feeling. The world, outside of Christ, operates entirely by the senses. The Lord Jesus declared the world would never receive the Holy Spirit because they could not see Him and understand Him by means of the natural senses.

Let us analyze this for just a moment. Can we know God by means of the senses? Have we ever seen God with the natural eye? Have we ever heard God speak through the natural ear? Have we felt Him with our hands? Has His presence ever been tasted or smelled? To all these questions the answer is, "No!"

God is made known only by the Holy Spirit who is given to us through the redemptive work of Jesus Christ on Calvary's cross. We know God in the inner man . . . NOT WITH THE OUTER. Through the senses we touch the world but not God.

When we talk about the world, we mean more than touching the ground, or seeing the sky, or living in our material houses. When the Bible speaks of the world it means "worldly affairs; the aggregate of things earthly; the whole circle of earthly goods, endowments, riches, advantages, pleasures, etc." All of these things can stir desire, seduce away from God, and be a device of Satan to render one spiritually impotent!

In which world do you live? What do you live for? What is your goal?

Today many people are making their world the world of sex and self gratification. They live as though sex might go out of style and they want to have as much of it as possible, now. They dress for sex. They earn money so that they might buy things which will eventually lead to sex, whether it be an apartment, automobile, hi-fi set, or what have you. This is the playboy world.

The Bible says this kind of world WARS against the soul. Peter said it this way,

"Abstain from fleshly lusts which WAR AGAINST THE SOUL."

(1 Pet. 2:11)

Paul said, "Your old nature . . . is corrupt through deceitful lusts." (Eph. 4:22) The nature which God gave man in the beginning was not corrupt but was corrupted through deceitful lusts. The desires of our instincts become lusts when they are drawn away from their natural functions and become ends in themselves. The self becomes egotistical; sex becomes sensuality; society and the demand for conformity become the god of our lives. This process corrupts the senses; our senses are not corrupt in themselves. They are God-made, God-ordained and God-blessed. But when we take them into our own hands, we set ourselves up as gods and that is the center of sin.

I hope I can make myself very clear here. THE REALM

123

OF THE WORLD IS THE REALM OF THE SENSES;
THE REALM OF THE SENSES IS THE REALM OF
INSTINCT. MAN WAS NOT CREATED TO BE LED BY
INSTINCT; MAN WAS CREATED TO BE LED BY
GOD.

THE REALM OF INSTINCT

When we deal with the realm or level of instinct, we are
involved with three drives: self, sex, and society. Instinct is
the level on which animals live. Man is not an animal so he
cannot live like an animal. Nature will not allow him to do
so no matter what the teachers of evolution might say. Man
cannot throw restraint to the winds and use sex without
inhibitions. Sex, even among animals, has inhibitions im-
posed upon them by nature. Man often attempts to live on
the level of instinct without the inhibitions of nature or social
morality, but this always runs him into difficulties.

On the level of man, we have the realm of MORAL LAW.
Animals survive as they respond to their physical environment. When they no longer are able to do so, they die. But
on the level of man, the secret of survival is not merely a
response to physical environment but to a moral environment as well, or he will perish.

This moral environment is not built by man in the form of
codes of conduct. It is built into the very nature of reality.
Break these laws, and you will be broken. Satan, our
adversary, knows this. So he attempts to blind our minds to
this truth that we might destroy ourselves and our effectiveness for God. As someone said, if you jump out of a ten-story
building, you do not break the law of gravity, you only
illustrate it! Anyone who tries to cheat a moral God, in a
moral universe, is a moral imbecile and derelict.

This introduction of moral law at the level of man puts restraints on the use of the three drives. When the devil showed Jesus the kingdoms of the world, he said: "It shall all be yours. if you listen to me and follow my ways." That phrase: "It shall all be yours," is the basis of all temptation against the SOUL—the temptation to find success by yourself or to find sexual fulfillment in a way other than God's way. Nothing is ours or is it real unless it is found in God.

Let me use sex as an illustration of my point. When sex is found in God, then sex finds itself fulfilled. When one man and one woman live together in moral faithfulness, a home is set up, children are born and love is the bond. That is sex—fulfilled and beautiful. But, suppose you listen to the lie that you can have sex apart from morality and apart from the way of God. What happens? You do not have sex; sex has you. It will dominate your thoughts and your actions. It will dominate you so completely, you become its slave. And when you become the slave of sex and soulish appetites, you find you have lost your creativity and your balance. In short, it will eat you up!

Not too many years ago, there were some psychiatrists who advised people who were disappointed in love and marriage, to free themselves from restraint and go out and find "your man" or "your woman." What happened? Did it cure the conflict? Far from it. It precipated a worse conflict!

Psychiatrists top the list as potential suicide cases!

"'The techniques that psychiatrists use to help their patients can cause the doctors to commit suicide,' a psychiatrist said recently.

"He contended that the professional requirement that a psychoanalyst undergo analysis is a major reason psychiatrists are more likely to kill themselves than men in any other profession.

"The self-knowledge a psychiatrist gains through analysis often brings to light elements in his personality that are difficult to live with.

"Over the last 70 years, at least 203 psychiatrists killed themselves. Over a third were under 40 years old." (Article by Boyce Rensberger, Detroit Free Press, 5/9/67)

Here, again, we have cases dealing with cases.

Today, more and more psychologists and psychiatrists are discovering man cannot resort to the level of the instincts to rid himself of frustrations. All must recognize sooner or later that when we come to the level of man we are introduced to a world of law and morality. This is how it is, LIKE IT OR NOT!

The moral universe and the Ten Commandments both say, "Thou shalt not commit adultery." Our inner being, made for this moral universe, chimes in and also says, "Thou shalt not commit adultery." The one who breaks this moral law is then in conflict with himself—inevitably. This is why we live in the age of the nervous breakdown. The sexually unmoral age coincides with the age of nervous breakdowns. Our hospitals and sanitariums are filled with people who thought they were free to break the moral law and found themselves free to break only themselves. Man cannot live like an animal. The moral law won't let him. He must come to terms with the moral law or he perishes.

One of the hardest things in life is to see young people ignore this fact and tell themselves they can live any way they please and get away with it. When you tell them they won't get away with it, it hurts to have them laugh in your face.

Just a few days ago my wife and I stopped at a restaurant for a bite of lunch as we were making some hospital calls. At one of the nearby tables, a mother and daughter were lunching together. In a short time two women acquaintances joined them. The conversation shifted from one subject to another. It was impossible for my wife and I not to hear it. The young lady was a college student. She told her mother and the other ladies about the intellectual people who had become such an important part of her world. As she was questioned by her mother and friends, she admitted she had been enticed to smoke marijuana. With this revelation, there came an uproar. The horrified mother lost her temper and her composure. When they were leaving and passed our table, she said, "Well, I'm modern, but this is going too far."

To most people being modern means being immoral to an average degree. But everyone who lives in immorality, soon learns it is its own punishment. To reap immorality in your own family is a difficult crop to harvest.

Immorality is a device of Satan in his war against the soul. If you give in to his temptations, you will loathe yourself, despise your personality, and be ashamed of the obvious change in your life.

"Abstain from fleshly lusts which war against the soul."

Immorality will ruin your effectiveness in the kingdom of God. It is not worth the price!

127

CHAPTER FOURTEEN

THE ORIGIN OF DEMONS

In Mark 16:16,17, the Bible says:

> "He that believeth and is baptized shall be saved; but he that believeth not shall be damned. AND THESE SIGNS SHALL FOLLOW them that believe; In my name shall they cast out DEVILS (DEMONS)."

What is a demon? Is this business of the existence of demons real, or is it sheer superstition which has been handed down to us from primitive man? Does the Bible teach the actuality of demons? From the Bible we will attempt to answer these and other related questions in this series of lessons.

The Bible certainly is not silent on the subject of demons and demon possession; far from it. It has much to say about this theme. The Scriptures are very vocal in their declaration of the reality of their existence. Demons are workers of evil. According to the Bible, evil is very real, a problem which is not an insignificant passing fad or one to be taken lightly. It is present with us.

Evil originated in the heart of Lucifer, the covering cherub of God. Rebellion and sin stemmed from him. We have to contend continually with evil. The powers of evil which are around us are difficult to explain apart from the clear teaching of the Bible. So let us resort to the Word of God for understanding of the subject. If we are to be men and women of God who know their right hands from their left hands, we must be thoroughly informed of our enemy's tactics and the evil he spreads.

THE EXISTENCE OF DEMONS

The Scriptures are emphatic in the fact there is a personal devil and there are demons. It is impossible to read the Bible, however lightly, and not be confronted with this strange phenomenon. According to the revealed Word of God, demons do exist. These words are found in James 2:19:

> "Thou believest that there is one God; thou doest well: the DEVILS (DEMONS) also believe and tremble."

Jesus certainly was very aware of the existence of literal demons, for He said:

> "In my name shall THEY CAST OUT DE-MONS."
>
> (Mark 16:17)

The nature of a demon is uncleanness. In the Bible, the terms, DEMON and UNCLEAN SPIRIT, are synonomous. We read in Luke 4:33:

> "And in the synagogue there was a man, which had a SPIRIT OF AN UNCLEAN DEMON, and cried out with a loud voice, saying, Let us alone;

what have we to do with thee, thou Jesus of Nazareth? art thou come to destroy us? I know thee who thou art; the Holy One of God." "And they were all amazed, insomuch that they questioned among themselves, saying, What thing is this? what new doctrine is this? for with authority commandeth he even the UNCLEAN SPIRITS, and they do obey him."

(Mark 1:27)

One point we must understand clearly is the use of the words, devil and demon, in the King James Version of the Bible. The word, devil, comes from the Greek word, "diabolos," meaning: "the slanderer or the accuser." When we use the word, "devil," we speak of the Prince of Evil, Satan. But, in the King James Version, we find the word devil is used also for lesser powers of evil, namely, demons. The words from which we derive our word DEMON, are: "dai-monium" or "dai-non." So, to distinguish the lesser powers of evil from the devil himself, it is best to use the word, DEMON.

Now that we are sure of the existence of demons, and that they are unclean in nature let us consider their activities.

According to the Scriptures, the activity of demons is to SEDUCE, PROMOTE DOCTRINES OF UNCLEAN-NESS, MAKE INFIRM, AND PROMOTE ERROR. We are told in 1 Timothy 4:1:

"Now the Spirit speaketh expressly, that in the latter times (the last days of this age) some shall depart from the faith, giving heed to SEDUCING SPIRITS, and DOCTRINES OF DEMONS; speaking lies in hypocrisy; having their conscience seared with a hot iron; forbidding to marry, and commanding to abstain from meats, which God hath created to be received with thanksgiving of them which believe and know the truth."

In Luke, chapter eight, we are shown a graphic picture of the infirming and tormenting work of demons.

"And they arrived at the country of the Gadarenes, which is over against Galilee. And when he (Jesus) went forth to land, there met him out of the city a certain man, which had DEMONS long time, and wore no clothes, neither abode in any house, but in the tombs. When he saw Jesus, he cried out, and fell down before him, and with a loud voice said, What have I to do with thee, Jesus, thou Son of God most high? I beseech thee, to torment me not, (For he had commanded the unclean spirit to come out of the man. For often times it had caught him: and he was kept bound with chains and in fetters; and he brake the bands, and was driven of the demon into the wilderness.) And Jesus asked him, saying, What is thy name? And he said, Legion: because many devils (DEMONS) were entered into him."

(26:30)

THE ORIGIN OF DEMONS

We have ample Scriptural proof of the fact of demons, who have a personal existence, an unclean nature, and the ability to seduce, infirm, and promote doctrines of demons. Now we want to know their origin.

In chapters three and four we learned how Lucifer (Satan)

rebelled against the Almighty. As a result of this insurrection, he was cast out of the mount of God. But, before he lost his place of authority, Lucifer incited a mutiny among the angelic hosts of heaven. When he fell, Lucifer did not fall alone. He took with him a great multitude of the lesser celestial beings. This we know from Matthew 25:41 and Rev. 12:3,4.

> "Then shall he say also unto them on the left hand, Depart from me, ye cursed, into everlasting fire, prepared for the devil and HIS ANGELS."

Here we are told distinctly that the devil (Satan) has with him a company of angels and there is a place of fire prepared for them by God. Revelation says:

> "And there appeared another wonder in heaven; and behold a great red dragon, having seven heads and ten horns, and seven crowns upon his heads. And his tail drew the THIRD PART of the STARS OF HEAVEN, and did cast them to the earth ... "

There is little doubt that the dragon which is described here is Satan. The drawing to himself of a third part of the stars (angels) of heaven speaks of the pre-adamic rebellion of Lucifer when Lucifer and his angels were cast down into the earth.

> " ... and the earth was without form and void, and darkness was upon the face of the deep."

> (Gen. 1:2)

133

Present in our world today, are angels who do the bidding of God in heaven and in earth. Also present, are those angels who rebelled with Lucifer and are called the FALLEN ANGELS. According to the Bible teaching, these fallen angels are divided into two classes: (1) those that are free, and (2) those that are bound. The angels who are free are abroad in the heavenlies moving under the direction of their prince-leader, Satan. These emissaries and subjects of Satan are called demons. Satan's angels and demons, are one and the same.

Satan's method of operation and his highly organized empire of roving spirits in the heavenlies is described in Ephesians 6:11,12.

> "Put on the whole armour of God, that ye may be able to stand against the wiles of the devil. For we wrestle not against flesh and blood, but against PRINCIPALITIES, against POWERS, against the RULERS OF THE DARKNESS OF THIS WORLD, against SPIRITUAL WICKEDNESS IN HIGH (heavenly) PLACES."

Satan's methods are described as WILES of the devil, while his organization is graduated as PRINCIPALITIES, POWERS, WORLD RULERS OF DARKNESS, and SPIRITUAL HOSTS OF WICKEDNESS IN THE HIGH AND HEAVENLY PLACES (super-terrestrial places).

SATAN'S LIMITATIONS

Satan's realm of power and operation is limited to the lower heavens. He CANNOT reach into the THIRD HEAVEN which is the PARADISE OF GOD. (2Cor. 12:2) Our ascended Christ is seated in the third heaven and Satan cannot enter there. We are told in Ephesians 1:21 that Christ has been,

> "... raised from the dead and (God) set him at his own right hand in the HEAVENLY PLACES, FAR ABOVE all principality, and power, and might, and dominion, and every name that is named, not only in this world, but also in that which is to come."

Satan and his demons are barred from the third heaven. He and his wicked satellites are confined to the first and second heavens. As "prince of the power of the air," he and his demons one day will be cast into a place called, "The Lake of Fire."

Do not confuse the two classes of fallen angels—those that are free (demons), and those that are bound. The fallen angels who are bound are described by Peter and Jude. Peter said,

> "For if God spared not the angels that sinned, but CAST THEM DOWN TO HELL, and DELIVERED THEM INTO CHAINS OF DARKNESS, to be reserved unto judgment."
>
> (2Peter 2:4)

Jude speaks also about the fallen angels who are bound.

> "I will therefore put you in remembrance, though ye once knew this, how that the Lord, having saved the people out of the land of Egypt, afterward destroyed them that believed not. AND THE

ANGELS which kept not their first estate, but left their own habitation, he hath RESERVED IN EVERLASTING CHAINS UNDER DARK-NESS unto the judgment of the great day."

(Jude 5,6)

From these two Scriptures we know there was a group of angels who were guilty of such horrible wickedness that they were not allowed by God to roam the heavenlies along with their leader Satan and the other evil angels. They were plunged into the strictest and severest confinement, into a place called, TAR-TAR-US, described as THE PITS OF DARKNESS. There they are being held, reserved unto the great day of judgment. This punishment came upon these fallen angels because "they kept not their first estate" but abandoned "their proper habitation."

We cannot connect this event with the original rebellion of Satan and the fall of his rebellious angels. Satan was not only the sole originator of that first insurrection, but the prime offender. We know, according to the Scriptures, Satan IS NOT NOW BOUND in chains under everlasting darkness. Presently he is free to roam through the heavens and the earth. This we learned in our study of the Book of Job.

In Genesis 6:1-6, we learn about the angels who left their estate and who now are bound in darkness and everlasting chains. Here is what happened:

"And it came to pass, when men began to multiply on the face of the earth, and daughters were born unto them, that the sons of God (angels) saw the daughters of men that they were fair; and they took them wives of all which they chose. And the Lord said, My spirit shall not always strive with

136

man, for that he also is flesh: Yet his days shall be an hundred and twenty years. There were GIANTS in the earth in those days; also after that, when the sons of God (angels) came in unto the daughters of men, and they bare children to them, the same became mighty men which were of old, men of renown. And God saw that the WICKED-NESS of men, was great in the earth, and that every imagination of the thoughts of his heart was only evil continually. And it repented the Lord that he had made man on the earth, and it grieved him at his heart."

This is one of the strangest Scriptures found in the Bible. But it clarifies what Peter and Jude said about the "angels who kept not their first estate," but did

"even as Sodom and Gomorrah, and the cities about them in like manner, giving themselves over to fornication and GOING AFTER STRANGE FLESH."

(Jude 7)

THE REASON FOR THE FLOOD

The Genesis account says there were certain of the angels who fell with Lucifer "who saw the daughters of men that they were fair." The angels lived with the women. They conceived and bare children whom the King James Version calls, GIANTS. The translator's use of the word "giant" here is unfortunate, because it has caused a great deal of confusion. The word from which "giant" was translated is the Hebrew word, "nephilim." This word comes from the root

137

word, "naphal," meaning, "to fall." So a better translation of the word, "nephilim," would be, THE FALLEN ONES, rather than "giants." This clearly means an unnatural off-spring of an unnatural union. It happened in the years before the flood and caused such terrible wickedness among man-kind, there was no alternative for God but to destroy the earth with a flood. Perhaps the thought in the mind of the ancient translators may well have been what we, today, would describe as "monsters," since their origin was not entirely human but a combination with the angelic.

These fallen angels who chose to leave their own realm and to break the bounds and God-ordained laws of two worlds to work havoc and vicious confusion in the earth, were wiped out by the flood. The results of their disorder was wiped out by God. They were dashed down into the lowest dungeons and deprived forever of any opportunity to cause further derangement.

There are some who strongly object to the thought of angels marrying humans on the basis of these words spoken by Jesus,

"The angels in heaven neither marry nor are given in marriage."

They conclude therefore, angels must be sexless. A careful examination of these Scriptures will bear out the fact that angels have no need to perpetuate their species through a marriage relationship because they are deathless. This Scrip-ture does not speak about angels being sex-less but rather they have no need to propagate. Remember also, Jesus was speaking here about the angels of heaven who minister in the light of the glory of God.

The New Testament definitely teaches that evil, unclean spirits (demons) can INHABIT THE BODIES OF MEN AND WOMEN to cause them to be rebellious, unclean and violent people. This is a strange yet very emphatic teaching in the Bible. Jesus taught these words:

> "When the unclean spirit is gone out of a man (this indicates the spirit once was IN the man), he walketh through dry places, seeking rest, and findeth none. Then he saith, I will return into my house from whence I came out; and when he is come, he findeth it empty, swept, and garnished. Then goeth he, and taketh with himself seven other SPIRITS more wicked than himself, and they ENTER IN and DWELL THERE: and the last state of that man is worse than the first."
>
> (Matt. 12:43–45)

This is stark reality. Consider carefully the facts stated here. Yes, demons are looking for human habitations. Then recognize that the Lord God has provided a place of safety for the true Christian, a hiding place—CHRIST JESUS, THE LORD.

CHAPTER FIFTEEN

UNDERSTANDING DEMON POSSESSION

What is a demon? A demon is a fallen angel who, with Lucifer in the beginning of the creation, rebelled against God, but who, unlike some fallen angels, did not leave his first estate or the bounds set by Almighty God.

A DEMON IS A SPIRIT BEING. This is definitely taught in the Scriptures. The Gospels of the New Testament prove conclusively that demons are solely spiritual beings. Here are some clear Scriptures to bear out this point:

> "When the even was come, they brought unto him (Jesus) many that were possessed with DEMONS: and he cast out THE SPIRITS with his word, and healed all that were sick."
>
> (Matt. 8:16)

> "And the seventy (disciples) returned again with joy, saying, Lord, even the DEMONS are subject unto us through thy name."
>
> (Lk. 10:17)

Jesus' answer was,

> "Notwithstanding in this rejoice not, that the

SPIRITS are subject unto you; but rather rejoice, because your names are written in heaven."

(Lk. 10:20)

The Bible makes it very plain that DEMONS and EVIL SPIRITS are one and the same.

The Apostle Paul confirmed this fact. He said:

"For we wrestle NOT AGAINST FLESH AND BLOOD, but against the non-material, the incorporeal—POWERS, PRINCIPALITIES, WORLD-RULERS OF THIS DARKNESS, AND SPIRIT-UAL HOSTS OF WICKEDNESS IN THE HEAVENLY PLACES."

(Eph. 6:12)

Of those outside of Christ, Paul said:

"Wherein in time past ye walked according to the course of this world, according to the prince of the power of the air, THE SPIRIT that now worketh in the children of disobedience."

(Eph. 2:2)

The "powers of the air" energize the ungodly; the Holy Spirit energizes the Godly!

Again I repeat: The Scriptures present DEMONS as purely spirit beings. There are several passages which tell what a spirit being is.

"God is spirit."

(Jn. 4:24)

"A spirit hath not flesh and bones."

(Lk. 24:39)

"Demons are spirits."

(Lk. 10:17,20)

"Angels . . . are spirits."

(Heb. 1:13,14)

We can conclude then the specific attribute of "spirit" is immateriality and incorporeality (without material or body).

Because demons are spirits, we must not think they are without personality. Demons, as well as all other created spiritual beings, possess personality, intelligence and volition. They are not subject to natural law and are not subject to human visibility or other sensory perception.

INTELLECTUAL IN NATURE

Demons are intellectual, of this there is no doubt. They knew very definitely that Jesus Christ was the Son of the Living God; they knew He was their Master; they knew they must obey Him. A very clear account of this is given in Mark 1:23,24:

"And there was in their synagogue a man with an unclean spirit; and he cried out, saying, Let us alone; what have we to do with thee, thou Jesus of Nazareth? art thou come to destroy us? I KNOW THEE who thou art, THE HOLY ONE OF GOD."

143

James says demons believe and tremble, or shudder. (Jas. 2:19)

The demons knew the Apostle Paul had been given authority over them. In acts 19:13–15, we have this account:

> "Then certain of the vagabond Jews, exorcists, took upon them to call over them which had EVIL SPIRITS the name of the Lord Jesus, saying, We adjure you by Jesus whom Paul preacheth. And there were seven sons of one Sceva, a Jew, and chief of the priests, which did so. And the EVIL SPIRIT answered and said, JESUS I KNOW, and PAUL I KNOW: but who are you?"

The demons KNEW Jesus, they KNEW Paul, and they KNOW THE BORN-AGAIN BELIEVER who has entered into a realm of power with God. Jesus said in the Great Commission:

> "He that believeth and is baptized shall be saved; but he that believeth not shall be damned. And these signs shall follow them that believe; In MY NAME shall they cast out demons . . . "
>
> (Mk. 16:16,17)

The believers' names are recorded in the heavenlies. The demons know this yet the vast majority of the born-again church people are being destroyed for their lack of knowledge.

MORAL IN NATURE

Just as demons have an intellectual nature, so also do they have a moral nature. It is described over and over again in

144

the Gospels and Acts as UNCLEAN! Demons are immoral. They entice people into immorality and uncleanness. Some people are harrassed constantly with unclean thoughts. They do not know it is a demon at work behind the temptation.

Demons are out to destroy, make no mistake about this! It is their nature to destroy. Their insidious power is behind all the violence and crime which is billowing over our country at the present time. Please do not hide your head in the sand by refusing to acknowledge the situation which now exists in our society. WE ARE IN THE THROES OF A CRIME WAVE CAUSED BY HATRED AND VIOLENCE. Evil spirits are inducing this and we had better do something about it!

The moral nature of demons is revealed by the afflictions they put upon people. They cause dumbness (Mt. 9:32,33), blindness (Mt. 12:22), insanity (Lk. 8:26,36), suicidal mania (Mk. 9:22), personal injury (Mk. 9:18), and various defects and deformities.

DEMON ACTIVITY

The main operation of both Satan and his demons is to OPPOSE GOD and THE WILL OF GOD IN MAN. Satan is what his name means—adversary, antagonist, enemy and foe. The other name used to identify him, "devil," means, "slanderer or accuser." These names describe his activities.

Today the devil still accuses God before man as he did with Eve when he said, "God is lying to you about that tree in the midst of the garden. If you eat of it, you will NOT die but you will BE AS GODS." Satan accused God of being deceitful!

The devil also accuses and slanders us before God just as he told God that Job was serving Him only for what he could get from Him. Satan's war is a war against the mind. It is an intrusion of his will against the divine will of God. This is how it was in the beginning; this is how it is today.

Satan opposes everyone and everything that is named by the Name of our God. However, since he is neither omnipresent, omnipotent, nor omniscient, the greater part of his colossal activity is carried on by his demons who have delegated realms of power and operations. Their goal: to distress mankind by deranging both body and mind by DEMON POSSESSION.

Before I delve into the topic of DEMON POSSESSION, let me assure you of this one thing—Satan and his demons only can operate under the permissive will of God. Demons are instruments by which God's plans are executed for punishing the ungodly. This fact is recorded in the Psalms where the Lord was speaking to Israel regarding the Egyptians.

"Yea, they turned back and tempted God, and limited the Holy One of Israel. They remembered not his hand, nor the day when he delivered them from the enemy. How he had wrought his signs in Egypt, and his wonders in the field of Zoan: and had turned their rivers into blood; and their floods, that they could not drink. He sent divers sorts of flies among them, which devoured them; and frogs, which destroyed them. He gave also their increase unto the caterpiller, and their labour unto the locust. He destroyed their vines with hail, and their sycamore trees with frost. He gave up their cattle also to the hail, and their flocks to hot thunderbolts. He cast upon them the fierceness of

his anger, wrath, and indignation, and trouble, BY
SENDING EVIL ANGELS AMONG THEM."

(Psa. 78:41–49)

Here we learn that the calamities which came upon Egypt
(sent by God) came as God allowed EVIL ANGELS to
descend upon the Egyptians. Actually, these demons can do
nothing except by God's permission and in God's time.

Another example of demons performing the will of God is
in the case of King Ahab. The record is found in 1Kings
22:20–22:

"And the Lord said, Who shall persuade Ahab,
that he may go up and fall at Ramoth-Gilead?
And one said on this manner, and another said on
that manner. And there came forth a SPIRIT, and
stood before the Lord, and said, I will persuade
him. And the Lord said unto him, Wherewith?
And he said, I will go forth, and I will be a LYING
SPIRIT in the mouth of all his prophets. And he
said, Thou shalt persuade him, and prevail also: go
forth, and do so."

Here we see men who were false prophets to Ahab,
themselves being deceived because they wanted to practice
deception. Again, an example of a demon performing the will
and purpose of God. Without knowing it, the kingdom of
Satan always has been divided against itself. FOR THIS
REASON IT CANNOT STAND. THE LORD GOD AL-
WAYS IS UNDERMINING SATAN WITH A WISDOM
WHICH BAFFLES HIM.

Satan and his ministers also effect God's plans for chastening the Godly who fall into sin. When Satan sifted Peter like wheat, he simply was accomplishing the Lord's purposes.

When Job was brought through the test induced by Satan, he was a better and more refined man of God.

A man in the Church at Corinth was living in sexual immorality with his stepmother. Paul's instructions to the church was,

> " . . . deliver unto Satan, this man, for the destruction of the flesh, that the spirit may be saved in the day of the Lord Jesus."
>
> (1 Cor. 5:5)

Again, God's plan was worked out by employing Satan's power.

Two ministers, Hymenaius and Alexander, also were "delivered unto Satan, that they might be taught not to blaspheme." (1Tim. 1:20)

We must have a respect for the powers of evil, but WE SHOULD NOT FEAR THEM. To fear them is to be subservient to them. The Lord must be our fear and our dread.

In the Name of Jesus Christ we are more than conquerors! Our God controls everything. He has established rigid bounds for Satan and his demons. Though Satan has great power, God has circumscribed his limitations. Beyond these, he may not go. He is permitted to employ an innumerable host of demons who are free to obey his behests, but he is not permitted to marshall ALL the evil agencies to concentrate their power to one design. God has set Satan's limits!

IF WE ARE IN CHRIST, Satan also is limited in his efforts against us when we die. Paul said to the Romans:

"For I am persuaded, that neither DEATH, nor life, nor ANGELS, nor PRINCIPALITIES, nor POWERS, nor things present, nor things to come, nor height, nor depth, nor any other creature, shall be able to separate us from the love of God, which is in Christ Jesus our Lord."

(Rom. 8:38,39)

For the man who is in Christ, there is security and safety. If you are wise, you will make certain you are HID IN HIM, WHO IS THE ROCK OF OUR SALVATION—the Lord Jesus Christ!

CHAPTER SIXTEEN

WHAT IS DEMON POSSESSION?

Probably no phase of Bible study has raised more speculation, or excited more doubt and skepticism, than the strange phenomenon of demon possession. To say the least, it is a very baffling theme.

Demon possession seems to be primarily a problem of the mind. The Bible is clear in its declaration that the mind of man is the focal point of Satan's major attacks. In speaking of people who are outside of Christ, Paul said:

> "But if our gospel be hid, it is hid to them that are lost: in whom the god of this world (Satan), hath BLINDED THE MINDS of them which believe not, lest the light of the glorious gospel of Christ, who is the image of God, should shine unto them."
>
> (2 Cor. 4:3,4)

Here the Scriptures distinctly tell us Satan can blind the minds of men so they are without understanding concerning the gospel of Christ.

We know also, it is possible for the mind of one human being to effect the mind of another. This is called mesmerism or hypnotism. Mesmerism is so-called because it was discovered by a man named F. A. Mesmer. This man first brought this to the attention of the public in Vienna, in about the year 1775. He learned that the mind of one person can not only influence the mind of another, but also can mesmerize, or hypnotize, or TAKE CONTROL, to such a degree as to impart to it a knowledge previously unknown.

THE HOLY SPIRIT

In contradistinction to the work of Satan against the mind of man to shut out spiritual light and to dominate one mind by another with hypnotism, is the tremendous work of the Holy Spirit within the Christian to illuminate and direct his mind.

One of the basic Christian tenets is that the Holy Spirit can indwell the bodies of believers and can act directly upon the minds of those who submit themselves to God's will. He inspires them with lofty aims and thoughts, guides them in the ways of righteousness, and leads them into ALL TRUTH.

Just as God, by the HOLY SPIRIT, influences the mind and direction of the Christian, so an EVIL SPIRIT can affect the mind, actions and directions of the ungodly.

A COMMON ERROR

Much skepticism arises from the common erroneous notion that demon possession was peculiar only to the time of Christ. It would be wonderful if this were true, but history makes us to know otherwise.

It cannot be denied that when Christ was ministering here on earth, there was an unusual and startling outbreak of demonism. According to the records of the gospels, it seems all the fury of the hosts of evil were concentrated against Jesus. There is little room for doubt about the existence of demons if one simply reads through the gospel accounts. For an example, take the gospel of Mark.

"And there was in their synagogue a man with an UNCLEAN SPIRIT, and he cried out, saying, Let us alone; what have we to do with thee, thou Jesus of Nazareth? art thou come to destroy us? I know thee who thou art, the Holy One of God. And Jesus rebuked him, saying, Hold thy peace, and come out of him. And when the UNCLEAN SPIRIT had torn him, and cried with a loud voice he came out of him. And they were all amazed, insomuch that they questioned among themselves, saying, What thing is this? what new doctrine is this? for with authority commandeth he even the unclean spirits, and they do obey him."

(Mark 1:23–27)

Talk about control of the mind? In this account the unclean spirit so possessed the man's mind and body, that the spirit spoke through him!

In Mark 1:32–34, we read:

"And at even, when the sun did set, they brought unto him all that were diseased, and them that were POSSESSED WITH DEVILS. And all the city was gathered together at the door. And he healed many that were sick of divers diseases, and cast out MANY DEMONS; and suffered not the DEMONS TO SPEAK, because THEY KNEW HIM."

"And he preached in their synagogues throughout all Galilee, and cast out DEMONS."

(Mark 1:39)

Such an eruption of demon power against the ministry of

153

Jesus should not be amazing for the coming of Christ was the inevitable clash of light and darkness. Jesus Christ came for the express purpose to "destroy the works of the devil." (1 John 3:8) It was His avowed intention to engage the enemy to defeat him, and to challenge his power to destroy it. With head-on impact, Jesus collided with Satan's fury and tyranny. It is not at all phenomenal that there was such an outburst of demonism at the coming of Christ. Rather, it would have been utterly surprising if such a manifestation had not taken place.

However, be well assured, cases of demon possession were not confined to Jesus' day. They have been constant down through history.

There is a popular and widespread belief that labors under the delusion there are no demons now because we live in an age of science and enlightenment. Through science and enlightenment, we receive the necessary answers for all the ills of mankind. This simply is not true. There are too many un-explainable problems around us to prove the shortcomings of science and enlightenment. Take just one look at our crime statistics. See how many people are crime repeaters. In spite of the best psychiatric care, they return to crime. What force is driving and compelling men to commit crime? Think a little about this. What force is behind the criminal mind? After being treated at hospitals and institutions, criminals return to their former activities. Why?

The Bible gives us the answer—evil powers are at work in the lives of men!

WHAT IS DEMON POSSESSION?

People who are demon possessed are incapable, at times, to separate their own consciousness and mental processes from the influence of a demon. Either they have lost it, or they have given up their free volition. There are times when their very thoughts are monopolized by a force and mind other than their own.

The Bible does not use the exact term, "demon possession," but the New Testament does speak of those having "a spirit, a demon, or an unclean spirit." Principally, this means people whom we would call, "demonized," meaning, they are suffering physical disease or mental derangement because they are controlled by demons or evil spirits.

VARIOUS SCHOOLS OF THOUGHT

Regarding demon possession, there are a number of theories. I will give you the three which are most popular, but I must say not one of them is scriptural.

THE ACCOMMODATION THEORY

The first of these is the "Accommodation Theory." It says Jesus simply accommodated the people of His day in their ignorance and superstition. Since they wanted to believe in demons, He simply allowed them to do so. He accommodated Himself to the beliefs of the people, knowing their belief in demons was only another way of expressing their belief in evil.

This theory of accommodation is exploded by an incident which happened after Jesus came dowm from the Mount of Transfiguration. A boy was brought to Jesus by a desperate father.

"And when they were come to the multitude, there came to him a certain man, kneeling down to him, and saying, Lord, have mercy on my son: for he is lunatick, and sore vexed: for ofttimes he falleth

155

into the fire, and oft into the water. And I brought
him to thy disciples, and they could not cure him.
Then Jesus answered and said, O faithless and
perverse generation, how long shall I be with you?
how long shall I suffer you? bring him hither to
me. And Jesus REBUKED THE DEMON; and
he departed out of him: and the child was cured
from that very hour."

(Mt. 17:14–18)

If the theory of accommodation were true, then Jesus
simply went along with the man's superstition and ignorance.
The man only was imagining his boy to be a lunatick, only
imagining a power within the boy wanted to destroy him by
throwing him into the fire and into the water. Jesus only
illustrated the principle of evil when he spoke to the demon
a word of rebuke which set the boy free.

This all was very real! Jesus was not accommodating
Himself to the ignorance of the people. That boy actually
was ruled by a demon.

THE MYTHICAL THEORY

The next theory I want to discuss is called, "The Mythical
Theory." This infers the whole Bible narrative of Jesus
casting out a demon was merely symbolic and without actual
foundation of fact. According to this theory, so-called demon
possession is but a vivid symbol of the prevalence of evil in
the world, and the casting out of demons by our Lord is only
a corresponding figure of triumph over evil by His doctrine
and life.

I think it would have been most difficult to convince the
farmers in the region of the Gadarenes who lost their swine

156

when they drowned in the sea that Jesus was only using the swine as a symbol of evil. The Bible account says Jesus cast a legion of demons out of a man and commanded them to go into a herd of swine which was grazing nearby. The herd numbered about 2,000. That is a good "mythical" number of swine to lose!

What did the keepers of the swine actually think of this "mythical" story? It was no myth to them; it was stark reality. They witnessed the deliverance and sanity of the one who had been demon possessed.

"And they that fed the swine fled, and told it in the city, and in the country. And they went out to see what it was that was done. And they come to Jesus, and see him that was possessed with the devil, and HAD THE LEGION, sitting, and clothed, and in his right mind: and they were afraid. And they that saw it told them how it befell to him that was possessed with the devil, and also concerning the swine. And they began to pray him (Jesus) to depart out of their coasts."

(Mark 5:14–17)

THE HALLUCINATION THEORY

The third theory is the "Hallucination Theory." Those who embrace this theory say those who were called "demon possessed" simply had worked themselves into a high emotional frenzy or mental excitement and relegated the pitch of emotions to the motivation of another force within them. This theory fails to explain how a person who is in such a state suddenly can identify Jesus Christ whom he has never seen or known.

"Let Us Make Man . . . "

The Scriptures tell us of a man who was a maniac who lived in Gadara. He was so violent, he could easily break chains, ropes and fetters. NO MAN COULD TAME HIM. He was like a beast. But when he saw Jesus,

> " . . . he ran and worshipped him, and cried with a loud voice, and said, What have I to do with thee, Jesus, thou Son of the most high God? I adjure thee by God, that thou torment me not."

(Mark 5:6,7)

This was no hallucination; this was real!

BIBLE TRUTH

A literal approach to the Bible record is the only sensible, logical answer to the phenomenon of demon possession.

How does one become demon possessed? Is that one accountable for his actions? These questions are often asked. I will do my best to answer them forthrightly and intelligibly.

HOW DOES A PERSON BECOME DEMON POSSESSED?

After a thorough search of the New Testament, I am convinced MOST people who become demon possessed are possessed because they have voluntarily yielded themselves to sin and iniquity, time and time again, until sin ruled over them. As a result of repeatedly committing sin and voluntarily yielding their members to sin, the human will is weakened to the point where the mind of that one becomes more and more susceptible to attackes of satanic forces. This causes a breakdown in the person's individualism. As more and more of the power of self-determination is lost, that one becomes more and more depressed and inactive. Sometimes these people are called, "maniac-depressive." Not only do they lose their power of self-determination but also the power of self-origination in mental and moral actions.

In other words, they have another voice prompting them from within which takes away more and more of the individual's self-initiative. Such people need help! Their problem is very real!

As Christians, we are under obligation to God to search out the Word of God that we be INFORMED people who can shed light to those in need of help. We are IN THE MIDST OF A CROOKED AND PERVERSE GENERATION, and if our gospel be hid, it is hid to them that are lost.

The place of safety against the attacks of Satan is in Jesus Christ. He is "our refuge and fortress, where the righteous run in and are safe." This is where you should be, and can be.

How can you be hid in Christ? Repent of your sin. Be baptized in the name of Jesus Christ for the remission of sins. Be filled with the Holy Spirit and you will have power to be a witness and an overcomer!

CHAPTER SEVENTEEN

CAN A BELIEVER BE
DEMON POSSESSED?

In considering the function of evil spirits, it is important we distinguish between (1) demon possession and demon control, and (2) demon influence. The New Testament gives ample warrant for such a distinction.

In speaking of demon possession, we believe the Bible teaches only UNBELIEVERS can be so exposed. But, in the matter of demon influence, both BELIEVERS and UNBELIEVERS can be involved.

In the case of demon possession, a person's personality actually is invaded, the body is inhabited, and a dominating control is gained. This actual possession is described in Matthew 12:43–45.

> "When the unclean spirit is gone out of a man, he walketh through dry places, seeking rest, and findeth none. Then he saith, I will return into my house from WHENCE I CAME OUT; and when he is come, he findeth it empty, swept, and garnished. Then goeth he, and taketh with himself seven other spirits more wicked than himself, and they ENTER IN AND DWELL THERE: and the last state of that man is worse than the first . . . "

These Scriptures are a graphic picture of a person who has

become possessed and inhabited by evil spirits. In Bible language,

> " . . . they ENTER IN AND DWELL THERE: and the last state of that man is worse than the first."

This can happen ONLY to those who do not belong to Christ.

DEMON INFLUENCE

However, as already has been mentioned, both the BELIEVER and the UNBELIEVER are open to demon INFLUENCE. What is Demon influence? It is Satan and his demons attacking from without by pressure, suggestion, and temptation through the avenue of the mind.

We have an excellent example of demon influence in the life of a believer—the Apostle Peter. On the same evening of His betrayal, the Lord Jesus turned to Peter and said,

> "Simon, Simon, behold, Satan hath desired to have you, that he may sift you as wheat: but I have prayed for thee, that thy faith fail not: and when thou art converted, strengthen thy brethren."
>
> (Luke 22:31,32)

By the permission of Jesus Christ, Satan moved in upon Peter to influence him. Satan could not POSSESS Peter, but he could strongly INFLUENCE his mind and spirit. Suddenly, Peter was unsure of himself. He was fearful of death and of being persecuted. He flatly denied he knew the Lord, not just once, but three times. Peter became weak and vacillating under the influence of Satan. But Satan could not possess Peter because he belonged to the Lord and the Lord Jesus was praying for him. Here is the account:

> "Then they took him (Jesus), and led him, and brought him into the high priest's house. And Peter followed afar off. And when they had kindled a fire in the midst of the hall, and were set down together, Peter sat down among them.
>
> "But a certain maid beheld him as he sat by the fire, and earnestly looked upon him, and said, This man was also with him. And he (Peter) denied him, saying, Woman, I know him not.
>
> "And after a little while another saw him, and said, thou art also of them. And Peter said, Man, I am not. And about the space of one hour after another confidently affirmed, saying, Of a truth this fellow also was with him: for he is a Galilaean. And Peter said, Man, I know not what thou sayest. And immediately while he yet spake the cock crew.
>
> "And the Lord turned, and looked upon Peter. And Peter remembered the word of the Lord how he had said unto him, Before the cock crow, thou shalt deny me thrice. And Peter went out, and wept bitterly."
>
> (Luke 22:54–62)

At one time Peter felt he was strong enough to stand against all the powers of Satan. Why, he had cast out devils and healed the sick! Though he thought himself to be very strong, he learned differently.

The reason the believer in Christ cannot be possessed of a demon, is he is Christ's purchased possession through redemption and the Lord is his master. Jesus said of His own (whom He called sheep),

> "My sheep hear my voice, and I KNOW THEM, and they follow me: and I give unto them eternal life; and they shall never perish, neither shall ANY pluck them out of my hand. My Father, which gave them me, is greater THAN ALL (Satan included); and no man is able to pluck them out of my Father's hand. I and my Father are one."
>
> (John 10:27–30)

PURCHASED POSSESSION

The true Christian has been purchased by the precious blood of Christ and, literally, has become the property of God. The Apostle Paul said to the Corinthian believers,

> "What, know ye not that your body is the temple of the Holy Ghost which is in you, which ye have of God, and YE ARE NOT YOUR OWN? For ye are bought with a price: therefore glorify God IN YOUR BODY, and in your spirit, which are (belong to) God's."
>
> (1 Cor. 6:19,20)

SEALED

Another reason Satan cannot possess the believer is, the believer is sealed with the Holy Spirit of promise when he finds Jesus Christ in true redemption. This is unto the day of redemption!

"And grieve not the Holy Spirit of God, whereby YE ARE SEALED UNTO THE DAY OF RE-DEMPTION."

(Eph. 4:30)

Though the believer perpetually is faced with the subtle power and cunning works of darkness, he can rest assured the conflict is from without. But there is something more every Christian must know. The Bible tells us the CHRISTIAN CANNOT WALK IN DISOBEDIENCE AND REBELLION AND GET AWAY WITH IT! Neither can the Christian walk in bitterness, wrath, anger, clamour and evil speaking and get away with it.

PSYCHO-SOMATIC PROBLEMS

So many who name the name of Christ are totally ignorant of the influence of Satan and his hosts against the human mind—the Christian included.

It is impossible for us to control the actions of others, but it IS POSSIBLE for us to control our own actions and attitudes. When someone transgresses against you, it is vital for you to control your reactions. YOU MUST FORGIVE QUICKLY lest bitterness or hatred take root. Get the matter settled as quickly as possible and dismiss it from your mind. If you do not do this, Satan will take occasion through your unforgiveness to begin a war of influence against your mind. Before long, your mind will be filled with resentment, clamour, evil speaking, etc. It is not long until the wrong attitudes develop a poison in the spirit. This then spreads throughout the body, effecting vital organs and causing definite sickness.

Thousands of Christians are passing the sicknesses of their minds and spirits to their bodies. In scientific terms, this is called a "psychosomatic problem." This means the problem is rooted in the mind and in the spirit, not in the body. The sickness had its origin from without, not from within. Once an individual opens the gate of the mind to bitterness and resentment, rest assured Satan will take advantage and aggravate that weakness until that one closes the door with confession and repentance.

In such cases, it is necessary for another believer who is STRONG in the Lord, to speak a word of rebuke against the tormenting, lying spirit at work against the mind of his brother. But this can be done only if the believer is prepared to lay down the war of bitterness and resentment and close the door against the enemy of his soul.

THE SIN UNTO DEATH

There is another realm of Satan's war against the believer which is important for all of us to know. All who have been born-again into the Kingdom of God should know about the SIN UNTO DEATH. It is mentioned in 1 John 5:16:

> "If any man see his brother sin a sin which is not unto death, he shall ask, and he shall give him life for them that sin not unto death. There is a SIN UNTO DEATH: I do not say that he shall pray for it."

The sin unto death is the sin of persistent disobedience and rebellion by a believer against the ways of God. When this happens, God, in His own time and in His own way, delivers such an one into the hands of Satan for the destruction of the body that the soul might be saved in the day of Jesus Christ. This, I am afraid, happens to many people. We can pray and pray, but nothing happens for the judgment of God has fallen.

This was the case of a man in the Corinthian church who persisted in a sin of uncleanness. He lived in sexual impurity with his step-mother. Finally, the church received these instructions:

> " ... deliver such an one unto Satan for the de-
> struction of THE FLESH, that THE SPIRIT may
> be saved in the day of the Lord Jesus."
>
> (1 Cor. 5:5)

Paul the Apostle also instructed the Corinthians it was very dangerous to come to the Communion Table and partake of the body and blood of the Lord if a man is living in persistent sin. He said:

> "Wherefore whosoever shall eat this bread, and
> drink this cup of the Lord, unworthily, shall be
> guilty of the body and blood of the Lord. But let a
> man EXAMINE HIMSELF, and so let him eat of
> that bread and drink of that cup. For he that
> eateth and drinketh unworthily, eateth and drink-
> eth damnation (judgment and chastening) to him-
> self, not discerning the Lord's body. FOR THIS
> CAUSE many are WEAK and SICKLY, and
> many SLEEP (die prematurely)."
>
> (1 Cor. 11:27–30)

The believer who sins does not become demon possessed. He finds himself in the hands of the living God who deals with him. The believer who is guilty of immorality, sensualism, or other gross sins, will find himself in trouble with God. I DO NOT WANT THIS TO HAPPEN TO ME!

I believe when God turns a believer over to Satan for the destruction of the flesh, it can mean many things. It may be exposure to demon influence, physical sickness, mental sickness, or premature physical death.

OTHER ASPECTS OF DEMON INFLUENCE

Demonic influence may assume a variety of forms when the Lord God turns a person over to Satan. One of these signs is a departure from the faith. Paul said to Timothy:

> "Now the Spirit speaketh expressly, that in the latter times some shall depart from the faith, GIVING HEED TO SEDUCING SPIRITS, and DOCTRINES OF DEVILS."
>
> (Tim. 4:1)

Other forms of demon influence are hypocrisy, uncleanness, corrupt doctrine, worldliness, division, and the like.

These are areas of Bible truth about which not much is heard. Good fundamentalists will teach that the believer cannot be possessed by demons of Satan, but they fail to tell about the results of not walking circumspectly before God. So the people are lulled into a false security, believing anything goes because they never will fall from grace. Well, falling from grace is one thing but falling into the hands of God is something else! I do not want to fall into the DISCIPLINING HANDS of Almighty God! I WANT HIS GRACE, NOT HIS DISCIPLINE.

The Lord God is not playing games with us. Redemption and the work of the church in the world are serious matters with God. He yet will have a church without spot or wrinkle, or any such thing. He will purify it, purge it, wash it with the water of His holy Word, and scourge it, if necessary.

" . . . serve God acceptably with reverence and godly fear: FOR OUR GOD IS A CONSUMING FIRE."

(Heb. 12:28,29)

The believer has complete safety as he walks in the light, as Christ is in the light, and shares in the wonderful fellowship which is ours in the New Covenant. His well-being of body, soul and spirit depends upon the maintenance of a strong and true relationship with the Lord.

CHAPTER EIGHTEEN

SONS BY ADOPTION

"For as many as are led by the Spirit of God, they are the sons of God. For ye have not received the spirit of fear; but ye have received the SPIRIT OF ADOPTION, whereby we cry, Abba, Father."

(Rom. 8:14,15)

These words of the Apostle Paul turn our attention to the fact that every TRUE BELIEVER is called to SONSHIP. Sonship means we are being led by the Spirit of God into areas of experience where we would never take ourselves. We are led by God and we follow without fear, because we have not received the spirit of bondage again to fear, but WE HAVE RECEIVED the Spirit of adoption. As a result we have the feeling of belonging, and cry, "My very own Father."

RESURRECTION LIFE

The believer in Christ is not to live in a state of fear because we have nothing to fear. We have been washed from our sins in the Blood of Christ; God's face is turned toward us in love; we have been buried with Christ in water baptism; we have risen with Him in newness of life. We are alive in God because of the GRACE of God.

171

It is a great tragedy that many people in the church do not know this truth in its fullest extent. So many, after meeting Christ, have fallen back under the yoke of legalism and legalistic religion. For, whenever there is legalism there must, of necessity, be the spirit of bondage to fear. It is heart-rending to read the history of the church and to find the constant return to the bondage of the law.

On the pages of the New Testament we discover that men followed Paul, from city to city, to tear down his preaching. When Paul arrived in a community, he proclaimed the doctrine of the Grace of God. He told the people if they would confess their sins to Christ, they could know their sins were forgiven and removed from them.

Paul left the cities after he had established a group of believers. The men, who were called Judaizers, who came from Jerusalem, told the believers they were mistaken. Surely, they would argue, a man must have some part in his salvation; his good works must have some place in the divine plan. So the poor babes in Christ turned their eyes away from the finished work of the cross, away from the open tomb and the ascension of Christ, to contemplate their own doings and what they yet must do. They wondered if they had done enough to merit God's acceptance. Right there they fell back into the spirit of bondage again to fear. They doubted their valid relationship to God through Christ, and thereby became totally unsure of this sonship.

SLAVE OR SON?

The contrast in our chapter Scripture is between the slave and the son. A believer who is in bondage can never render anything more than the service of a slave. But the one who is truly joined to Christ has been brought into the position where it is possible for him to render the service of a SON. It is absolutely necessary for us to know our relationship and position in God. Our state of security in the position of sons determines the rate of our growth of power, responsibility, and authority which is ours through our oneness with Christ.

God does not want His children to be in fear. We must know, as the children of God, that our Lord does not deal with us in wrath but in mercy. The Spirit of God, which is the Holy Spirit, does not inspire fear in the heart of the believer. The Holy Spirit working in our heart gives a constant awareness that we have access to God, and He delights to have us in His presence. The Christian is never to tremble with fear or to be tormented with anxiety.

On the contrary, God's wrath is stilled in our regard. We have been begotten to divine sonship and adopted into an official position into the family of God. With this knowledge in our hearts and minds, we can turn to our Heavenly Father with utter calmness and with full confidence that He cannot and will not turn us away. All this is involved in our position. All this is guaranteed in our sonship.

THE SPIRIT OF ADOPTION

It is very important for us to understand fully what is meant by the SPIRIT OF ADOPTION. There has been a great deal of confusion in this matter because of a failure to understand the meaning of the word "adoption," as it is used in the New Testament. Some students of the Bible have confused adoption with the "new birth," not realizing that adoption had nothing to do with our coming into the family of God. Adoption is something much greater and more wonderful. (One must first be born to be adopted!)

Since the subject of adoption is very foggy to most people,

173

I want to take a little time to acquaint you with what it really is.

In olden times, adoption was as follow.

> "These effects have to do with private right and with public and religious right. As to private right, there was for the one who was adopted a change of family, but only so far as the paternal (father's) branch was concerned; the civil bonds which united the adopted one to his father and his father's relatives were broken; but the adopted one kept all his rights in his maternal (mother's) family: it was impossible to leave the mother's family by the law of adoption. The one who is adopted becomes the legitimate and necessary heir of the one who adopts him. This quality of heir, much deeper among the Greeks than among the Romans or in modern legislation, implied the most complete continuation of the person of the deceased; this the adopted one acquired as elements of his inheritance, not only the property but also the name of the deceased, all his rights of relationship, his dignities and honors, and, as well, succeeded to his judgments and debts. Upon the adopted one fell the responsibility for all minor children subsequently born to the one who adopted him."
>
> (Dictionnaire des Antiquites)

THE MEANING OF ADOPTION

The Greek word which is translated as "adoption" in our King James Bible, has a deeper meaning that our general understanding of the word. The Greek word is "huiothesia."

The first half is "huios," the common noun for an ADULT son. The latter half of the word, "thesia," means a placement, an installation, a setting of a person or a thing in its place. So the whole word means not so much the procedure of adoption with which we are familiar, but it actually means the PLACING OF A SON.

At one time in the Roman Empire it became the custom for men to have a ceremony in which their own sons were acknowledged publicly. This is the sense in which the Bible uses the word "adoption" in Romans 8. It is NOT the adoption of a child into another family, but the welcoming of a child into full-grown manhood. We could say we have not received the spirit of bondage again to fear, but we have received the spirit of a SON COME OF AGE WHO IS PUBLICLY ACKNOWLEDGED BY HIS FATHER.

This same thought is recorded for us in Gal. 4:1–3, 6,7.

> "Now I say, That the heir, as long as he is a CHILD, differeth nothing from a servant, though he be lord of all; but is under tutors and governors until the time appointed of the father. Even so we, when we were children, were in bondage under the elements of the world: ...and because ye are sons, God hath sent forth the Spirit of His Son, into your hearts, crying, Abba, Father. Wherefore thou art no more a servant, but a son; and if a son, then an HEIR OF GOD through Christ."

ABBA FATHER

When the Holy Spirit implants within the child of God the Spirit of adoption, He leads him to pray, and say, "Abba, Father." We pray and live like people who have the full acknowledgment of God's absolute right to make the way of approach to Himself in the way He desires. That approach is ONLY and ALWAYS through Jesus Christ.

The failure to understand this truth causes people who are RELIGIOUS without being truly Christians to be frustrated in their religious lives. They pray. Sure, they do. But the heavens are brass above them. NEVER, throughout their entire lives do they have the sense or feeling of getting through to God. Adoption brings a sense of security and the inner feeling of belonging. This, most religious people never really have. Why? Because they have not experienced true spiritual birth, and therefore, cannot experience true spiritual growth. They never learn because they refuse to submit to the discipline of God. They live their own religious way which is not God's way.

Being sure of your relationship to God is the greatest possible knowledge in this life. This knowledge gives poise and power to the Christian. I feel deeply worried for the person who is never quite sure he is really accepted of God.

"The spirit of adoption," as it is mentioned in the Epistle to the Romans, is called in Galatians, "the Spirit of His Son," meaning the Spirit of Christ. When we examine carefully the life and Spirit of Jesus, we see a man walking confidently before the Father. The Father had made a public declaration concerning Jesus. He said, "This is my beloved SON, in whom I am well pleased." Jesus knew He had access to the Father, and that they were one in Spirit. This is why Jesus was so sure of His ground wherever He went. The religious people of Jesus' day were scandalized by His associations. They said, "This man receives sinners and eats with them." But that complaint became a compliment. For, when Jesus received sinners, they didn't remain sinners—they became saints. They, too, learned to know the Lord God as their Father.

To know God in His fullness you must throw yourself unreservedly upon His grace and mercy. Do not set out to earn a position of sonship and authority with God. You will never make it that way and will end up discouraged and frustrated.

THE PRODIGAL SON

I think about the parable of the prodigal son. His elder brother represents the attempts at fellowship and sonship with the father on the basis of work and merit. He said to his father,

> "I never disobeyed your command; yet you never gave me a kid, that I might make merry with my friends. But when this son of yours came, who has devoured your living with harlots, you killed the fatted calf."

This older son could have had these same things at any time if he had wanted them and asked for them. But, evidently, he wasn't sure if he had done enough to deserve them. The younger son received them all simply because he returned to his father, to the place where he knew he belonged. By coming on the merits of grace, everything was opened to the younger son—the father's arms, the feasting, the rejoicing, and the reconciliation. The parable ends with the one who tried to earn the fellowship with the father sulking on the outside, and the one who took the fellowship through grace, rejoicing in the home with the father.

God has provided salvation and sonship for you. Why don't you take it?

All religions of the world fall into just two classes— salvation as by the work of man, or salvation as a gift of

God—self-salvation or God-salvation. There are no other types. All fall into one class or the other. They did so in ancient times; they do so today.

Jesus has provided our great salvation through His cross. He will lead you to sonship if you will stop placing yourself under more and more bondage. Accept what He has done for you. It is a complete salvation. Stop striving. Allow the Holy Spirit to come into your heart to enable you to say, "Abba (my very own), Father."

When the Lord God places you as a son, and you receive the Spirit of adoption, you know it! The coming of the spirit of adoption, in a sense, marks the beginning of maturity for the believer.

Judaism practices what is called "the BAR MITZVAH." Circumcision marks the infant's initiation into the Jewish fold. Bar Mitzvah, 13 years later, symbolizes the beginning of maturity for the boy. It is believed that until the thirteenth year, the father bears the sins of his son. After that, the boy is responsible for this own good or evil deeds and actions.

In christianity, we must all strive toward full-grown sonship. How are you maturing? I sincerely hope you have the feeling of belonging, a "son" consciousness.

CHAPTER NINETEEN

CHILDREN OF GOD

In the last chapter we used the theme verse of Romans 8:14,15.

> "For as many as are led by the Spirit of God, they are the sons of God. For ye have not received the spirit of bondage again to fear; but ye have received the Spirit of Adoption, whereby we cry, Abba, Father."

We learned that New Testament adoption means THE PLACING OF SONS by God Himself, and the beginning of a walk toward maturity.

In this lesson I will minister on the inner witness of the Holy Spirit (within the Christian) which causes him to know he is a child of God. The theme verse for this lesson is Romans 8:16.

> "The Spirit himself beareth witness with our spirit, THAT WE ARE THE CHILDREN OF GOD."

To know what and whom we are in God cannot be emphasized too much nor can its importance be stressed too strongly for we cannot be effective in the Kingdom of God unless we have this knowledge. We dare not be half-sure. We

179

must know without a doubt whether or not we are the children of God.

Our theme Scripture tells us we can know we are the children of God by an inner witness of the Holy Spirit. Can this inner witness be trusted? Is the inner witness enough? Many people down through history have said they were directed by God through an inner voice, but time proved they heard nothing, heard the voice of Satan, or heard the voice of their own imagination. Usually it was the latter.

How can we be sure?

The Scriptures tell us there is a definite way of knowing whether or not the Spirit of God has spoken to us. We know whether it be God if what our spirit says agrees with the WORD OF GOD. The Bible says:

> "For there are three that bear record in heaven, the
> FATHER, the WORD, and the HOLY GHOST:
> and these three (agree) are ONE."

> (1 John 5:7)

This means what God the Father speaks, and what the Holy Spirit administers, is ALWAYS in agreement with the Bible.

The effective Christian is a person who knows what he has experienced and what the Word of God says about THAT EXPERIENCE.

Take, for example, this Scripture:

> "He that believeth and is baptized shall be saved."
> (Mark 16:16)

When a person obeys the Word of God and repents before God, believing he is heard and forgiven, and is baptized, something happens. That something is the inner witness of the Holy Spirit in his heart which causes him to know the sin question has been resolved. He knows he has firm ground upon which to stand because the WORD OF GOD AND THE SPIRIT AGREE, giving witness that he is accepted of God.

THE WITNESS OF MEN

To know the Spirit of God is witnessing to truth is a wonderful and glorious experience. The Bible distinctly teaches there is a witness of the Holy Spirit and there is a witness of men. These words are found in 1 John 5:9.

"If we receive the witness of men, the witness of God is greater: for this the witness of God which he hath testified of his son."

Think about the witness of men for just a moment. This morning while you sat at the breakfast table, you read the morning newspaper. You saw an advertisement of something you have wanted to buy. Did you believe that ad? Did you believe that information presented to you on that printed page? Of course you did. Why did you believe it? I will tell you why. Because you have learned you can believe men and women around us. We act upon the information they give us because we receive their witness and believe it.

THE WITNESS OF GOD

The Bible says the witness of men is good, but the WITNESS OF GOD IS GREATER. One of the mysteries of life is why we will so gullibly believe men, who are born liars, and not believe God who cannot lie. We believe strangers, radio announcements, television commercials, newspaper reports, and printed labels on medicine bottles, while at the same time we reject the clear Word of God.

THE CONFUSION

I believe the reason so many people are unsure regarding the salvation of the Lord is they do not understand the witness of God. The witness of God is always at least TWO-FOLD. I have heard many good, zealous people endeavor to convince someone to believe in Christ on the basis of the Word of the Bible alone. This cannot be done. Let me illustrate what I mean.

At the close of many services an altar call is given, or an invitation to come to Christ and confess our sins to Him. When a person responds, an altar worker approaches him and gives him instructions to confess his sins and say, "God be merciful to me a sinner." When this simple instruction is followed, many sense the presence of God and the glorious realization that the Lord has rolled away the burden of sin. They rise from their knees with their consciences relieved of guilt.

But, sad to say, others seemingly do the same thing yet sense nothing. They tell the worker so. Then, some uninformed people will begin to try to convince these seekers that they are children of God because the Bible says so. They will recite one verse after another to convince the seekers to mentally accept the work of salvation. THIS IS NOT ENOUGH.

Too many people have mentally acquiesced to this kind of ritual and have no inner assurance of forgiveness or acceptance. When we have truly repented, and that repentance has been accepted by God, there comes this marvelous inner witness of the Holy Spirit which causes us to know we truly and genuinely are children of God. When the witness of the

Spirit is genuine we will be led into further truth. We will desire water baptism, and also will desire to be filled with the fullness of the Holy Spirit.

I am inclined to strongly doubt the genuineness of the operation of the Holy Spirit in the life of a person where there is no continuance, no hunger, and no desire for more of the glorious realities in God.

The witness of the Holy Spirit is such that it draws us into the center of life with Christ. It makes us conscious of our union with Him in His eternal plan for us. Our union with Him is climaxed in His death and resurrection. This is what sets the heart to such rejoicing with the God who did all of this, that we joyfully cry, "Abba, Father."

THE WITNESS TO PAUL AND SILAS

It is my firm belief that this inner witness continues and increases in the life of the true believer. Especially in the rough, hard spots in life, this inner witness gives assurance in the midst of trials, God has not deserted us. I am sure this is why Paul and Silas sang at midnight when they were in the Philippian jail. The Bible says:

> "And at midnight Paul and Silas prayed, and SANG PRAISES UNTO GOD: and the prisoners heard them. And suddenly there was a great earthquake, so that the foundations of the prison were shaken: and immediately all the doors were opened, and everyone's bands were loosed."
>
> (Acts 16:25,26)

What prompted Paul and Silas to sing praises when they were in prison, and were committed there unjustly? They had the inner witness they were the children of God.

183

They did not need to be in church to have the feeling they belonged. They knew Christ was with them wherever they were. They were sons of God in the midst of a crooked and perverse generation. They also knew Christ would never leave and never forsake. What a knowledge! Wouldn't you like to have it?

I heard someone say when Paul and Silas began to sing praises, the Lord God could not resist the desire to come down and sing with them. And when God added the bass notes to this duet, the prison began to shake and tremble. Be that as it may, God was there, and Paul and Silas knew it.

It should make no difference where we are, as long as we have the assurance God is there!

If you really belong to the Lord and have learned to trust in Him alone, that divine voice and witness of the Holy Spirit rings within you giving the warm glow of divinely revealed truth. Within your heart there is a melody.

WITH OUR SPIRIT

Notice the Bible does not say the Holy Spirit bears witness TO our spirits that we are the children of God, but He bears witness WITH our spirits. It is an inner conviction we have passed from death unto life.

The phrase BEARETH WITNESS WITH means the Holy Spirit adds His testimony to the testimony of the life and the truth at work within us. A depth of divine worship is ours along with the sense of divine presence.

MAN'S INNER BEING

How does the Holy Spirit communicate His testimony within Us? When the Scripture says the Holy Spirit bears witness with our spirit, what is meant by "our spirit?"

Man was created body, soul, and spirit by the hand of God. The Bible story of the creation simply states,

> "the Lord God formed man of the dust of the ground, and breathed into his nostrils the breath of life; and man became a living soul."
>
> (Gen. 2:7)

Adam and Eve had bodies which were created by God. They themselves were said to be souls, and they received spirits from the Creator. Bodies have five senses. Through these senses we have consciousness of the world about us. We hear, see, taste, touch, and smell. These sensory perceptions are translated by our brains for use by the inner man, the soul and the spirit. The SOUL makes man SELF-conscious; the SPIRIT makes man GOD-conscious; the BODY makes man WORLD-conscious.

Before Adam fell in sin he was very God-conscious. Adam's soul was his "ego," his self. The center of the will, we are told, is the soul. Here man makes his decisions governing his actions.

A man who is only self or soul conscious, makes all his own decisions and decides all his own actions. If a man is God-conscious, he will allow the Lord God to lead him into the right and proper decisions. When Adam sinned he placed his own will (his soul) in a seat above his spirit, and deliberately rebelled against the will of God. With this rebellion, sin came into the world. If Adam had yielded himself to God, the Lord God could have spoken to him and told him what was right in that given situation. But Adam did not.

The problem with unredeemed man is he has no inner

consciousness of the presence of God and, therefore, faces life alone. The Christian has become inwardly aware of the witness of God. This witness is intensified as he continues to walk with God.

Do you know there are millions of people in this nation who do not have the inner consciousness of the real presence of a living God? They are religious, but because they have not been born of the "water and the Spirit", they are not God-conscious. This is tragedy!

If you have truly found repentance and made your way to Christ, His Spirit will bear witness with your spirit that you are a child of God. You will be God-conscious.

CHAPTER TWENTY

HEIRS AND JOINT HEIRS

We are learning what it means to be a true child of God, realizing God's great plan and purposes involved.

In this lesson, I want to deal with the tremendous subject of being HEIRS OF GOD, JOINT HEIRS WITH JESUS CHRIST. We find the following words in Romans 8:17:

"And if children, then heirs; heirs of God, and joint-heirs with Christ; if so be that we suffer with Him, that we may be also glorified together."

Think about these verses and what they mean. IF we have become the children of God, then we are HIS HEIRS. IF CHILDREN, THEN HEIRS! Heirship depends entirely upon our relationship with God. If we have been born of God, "born-again," we have become children of God and consequently heirs of the Almighty. This is a part of the great and wonderful purpose of God in redemption.

ALL BY GRACE

Becoming an heir of God is the Lord's doing. By His grace and mercy alone we are given such glorious privileges. Seemingly, one of the hardest lessons for man to learn is that everything God does for him IS BY GRACE. Man is so eager to have some credit for his blessings it is difficult for him to admit his complete spiritual bankruptcy and utter dependency upon God. In fact, this one thing, more than anything else, keeps men from receiving God's wonderful visitations. We will not admit we are spiritually bankrupt.

This generation is so empty yet is endeavoring to convince itself it is full. What fools we are! Why is it so difficult for us to acknowledge the fact that God in His Sovereign love stooped down to a lost race which could not help itself. It was dead in trespasses and sins, totally responsible yet totally incapable of doing anything about it. God decided to quicken some of His creatures and make them HIS SONS.

One of the great mysteries of the grace of God is that God quickens some to sonship but does not quicken others. Why, I do not know. Bible facts confirm this. There is nothing good in any of us which could recommend us to God. Then, since God makes a division in the human race (and He does), He must do it on some principle found in Him and in Him alone. God does not work according to whim and fancy, but according to divine plan and purpose.

We do not climb up to God, but God reaches down to us and quickens our lost souls.

THE INHERITANCE

In dealing with the plan of God, we deal with grace and grace alone. When the Lord God saved us from our sins, it was His delight to make us His heirs. And heirship always implies an inheritance. If we are made heirs, we become partakers of the inheritance left us at the death of the testator. So, as the designated heirs of God, the Christian has become a partaker of a divine inheritance which is by grace. It comes with the divine sonship, and is ours because our

Lord died. In the epistle to the Hebrews, we read of the method whereby the inheritance of the Lord was secured for us.

First, the Lord Jesus came into the world as our great HIGH PRIEST. By His coming, He replaced all other priests and opened up a NEW and LIVING way into the presence of God that can never be closed. By His death, burial, and resurrection, He became the MEDIATOR OF THE NEW COVENANT. No other mediator is needed for any man. Christ is the one mediator between the soul of a man and God.

In the Old Testament, the way to God was kept open by a priesthood which killed sacrificial animals, shedding their blood as a picture of the death of the Lord Jesus. The Hebrew writer says:

"How much more (than these animal sacrifices) shall the blood of Christ, who through the eternal Spirit offered himself without spot to God, purge your conscience from dead works to serve the living God? And for this cause he (Jesus Christ) is the mediator of the new testament (covenant), that by means of death, for the redemption of the transgressions that were under the first testament (covenant), they which are called might receive the promise of ETERNAL INHERITANCE."

(Heb. 9:14,15)

Notice the writer tells us that through His death, Christ became the mediator of the NEW COVENANT. And those who are called into this new covenant relationship as the children and sons of God, are given the promise of an ETERNAL INHERITANCE. Consider the word ETER-

"Let Us Make Man ..."

NAL. This inheritance is not a ten, twenty, or fifty year
inheritance; it is an ETERNAL inheritance. We will share
the goodness and blessings of God in Christ throughout
eternity.

The writer goes on to say next:

> "For where a testament is, there must also of
> necessity be the death of the testator."
>
> (Heb. 9:16)

Nothing is truer than this Bible verse. A will is worth
nothing until the person who made the will has died. This is
how our eternal inheritance has come to us. The Lord Jesus
Christ loved us. That we might have all things in Him, He
died. Now our inheritance has been made sure. Thank God,
that there might be no question about our inheritance, He
arose from the dead to become the executor of His own
estate!

I have read accounts where an executor squandered an
estate and the heirs were cheated of their rightful inheritance.
This cannot possibly happen to the truly born-again Christian for Jesus Christ ever liveth to make sure the inheritance
goes to all the rightful heirs.

In my opinion, Hebrews 7:25 is one of the greatest verses
in the entire Bible. It tells me of the sure place which is mine
in God, through Christ.

> "Wherefore he (Jesus Christ) IS ABLE also to save
> them to the uttermost that come unto God BY
> HIM, seeing he ever liveth to make intercession for
> them."

Jesus Christ ever lives to make our inheritance sure!

190

JOINT-HEIRS

Our theme verse tells us beyond being an heir of God, we are joint-heirs with Christ.

The laws designate a difference between an heir and a joint-heir. The distinction is not difficult to understand. If a man dies and leaves a large estate to four heirs, the estate is divided evenly among them. Each heir received 25 per cent of the whole. But, if a man leaves an estate to four of his sons as joint-heirs, then each son owns the whole farm. Each one can say, "That house is mine; those barns are mine; those fields are mine."

So when the Lord tells us we are heirs of God and joint-heirs with Jesus Christ, we are being informed that everything God the Father has given to the Lord Jesus Christ has been given to us. I'm sure some of you are saying this is too much. It is too good to be true. But this is precisely what the Bible teaches. As joint-heirs with Christ, we are to share in all the Father has given Him,

This being true, we want to search out, in the Bible, those things that are a part of our future, and a part of our joint-heirship.

JUDGMENT

Let me state that the Bible teaches Jesus Christ is coming to this earth again. We call His coming the "second coming of Jesus Christ." Our Lord Jesus Christ is now seated in the heavens at the right hand of the majesty of God. He will remain there until the restoration of all things occurs as spoken by the mouth of all of God's holy prophets since the world began (Acts 3:21). But the day will come, in the economy of God, when our Lord will rise from the throne of

His heavenly mediation, lay aside the robes of His high-priestly ministry, and will descend from heaven with a shout and the voice of the archangel and the trump of God. At the time of His coming there will be a great resurrection of those who are in Christ at this time.

The Bible teaches that when Christ comes the second time, He will come to bring JUDGMENT and BLESSING. His coming in Judgment is described in Psalms 2:6–9.

> "Yet I have set my King upon my holy hill of Zion . . . Ask of me, and I shall give thee the nations for thine inheritance, and the uttermost parts of the earth for thy possession. Thou shalt break them with a rod of iron; thou shalt dash them to pieces like a potters vessel."

Notice the words that the Father has put the nations into the hands of His son. The day will come when He will sit in judgment upon the nations, and shall rule and break them with a ROD OF IRON.

In the Book of Revelation, we are told how the redeemed of God will share in this judgment of the nations as joint-heirs. Ruling, reigning, and judging with Him is an integral part of our spiritual inheritance.

> "And he that overcometh, and keepeth my words unto the end, to him will I give POWER OVER THE NATIONS; and he shall rule them WITH A ROD OF IRON; as the vessels of a potter shall they be broken to shivers; even as I received of my Father."
>
> (Rev. 2:26,27)

Think of it! It is the purpose and plan of the Almighty God that His sons rule and reign with Christ over the nations.

GOVERNMENT

The second area of joint-heirship is in government. The teaching of Jesus regarding future government is found in Matthew 25:31–34.

> "When the Son of man shall come in his glory, and all the holy angels with him, then shall he sit upon the throne of his glory; and before him shall be gathered ALL NATIONS: and he shall separate them one from another, as a shepherd divideth his sheep from the goats: and he shall set the sheep on his right hand, but the goats on the left. Then shall the King say unto them on his right hand, Come, ye blessed of my Father, inherit THE KINGDOM prepared for you from the foundation of the world."

At the present time, the Lord Jesus is seated at the right hand of the Father in the heavenlies. At a future time the Lord Jesus will have His own throne, and we shall share that throne of government WITH Him. The expression of joint-heirship in government is found in Revelation 3:21.

> "To him that overcometh will I grant TO SIT WITH ME IN MY THRONE, even as I also overcame, and am set down with my Father in His throne."

JOINT-HEIRS OF ALL THAT HE HAS

We are joint-heirs of all that He has, as well as fellow-participants in all that He does. Christ delights to share with us all that He now possesses. Listen to these New Testament verses.

> "Blessed by the God and Father of our Lord Jesus Christ, who hath blessed us with ALL SPIRITU-AL BLESSINGS in heavenly places in Christ."
>
> (Eph. 1:3)

> The blessings of Christ which are His as He sits in the heavenly places with the Father are now to be shared with us through the mercy and grace of our God.

> Is the Lord our God rich? Does He want to share His vast riches with us? The Bible says He does.

> "Ye know the grace of our Lord Jesus Christ, that, though he was rich, yet for your sakes he became poor, that YE through his poverty MIGHT BE RICH.
>
> (2 Cor. 8:9)

JOINT-HEIRS OF ALL THAT HE IS

We are also joint-heirs with Christ of all that He IS. Name any of the divine attributes, and you will discover the Word of God promises that same attribute to all who are in Christ. Do you marvel at the wisdom of Christ? The Bible says:

"Christ Jesus ... is made unto us wisdom."

(1 Cor. 1:30)

Paul tells the Corinthians,

"Now I know in part; but then (when the Lord comes to complete the work of our glorification) shall I know even as I am known."

(1 Cor. 13:12)

Have you thought of the divine power of Christ and ever wondered if we possibly can have a share in it? It is possible! Today we can say,

"I can do all things through Christ which strengtheneth me."

(Phil. 4:13)

If we can say this now, how much more shall we realize the Lord's power when we shall be made like Him.

And, how about His holiness? The Bible says as joint-heirs we become partakers of His HOLINESS. This holiness is not the outward kind a man can manufacture. It is an inner holiness, an inner setting apart unto God by the work and power of the Holy Spirit. I receive great assurance from the words of 1 Cor. 1:30,31.

"But of Him are ye in Christ Jesus, who of God is made unto us wisdom, and righteousness, and sanctification, and redemption: that, according as it is written, he that glorieth, let him glory in the Lord."

195

"Let Us Make Man . . ."

Consider our theme text again.

"If children, then heirs: HEIRS OF GOD AND
JOINT-HEIRS WITH CHRIST."

All these things belong to the true believer in Christ. Let
us make sure we are not missing God's best because of lack
of knowledge!

CHAPTER TWENTY-ONE

SUFFERING AND GLORY

"For I reckon that the sufferings of this present time are not worthy to be compared with the glory which shall be revealed in us. For the earnest expectation of the creature waiteth for the manifestation of the sons of God. For the creature was made subject to vanity, not willingly, but by reason of him who hath subjected the same in hope, because the creature itself also shall be delivered from the bondage of corruption into the glorious liberty of the children of God."

(Romans 8:18–21)

There is little doubt in the mind of anyone who has walked with God for any length of time that there are sufferings which are common to the whole of the human race, and there are other sufferings peculiar only to believers in Christ. In the more mature stages of the Christian life, sufferings are experienced which are completely unknown to the new-born child of God.

COMMON SUFFERINGS

The sufferings which are common to the whole human race have been in the world since the entrance of sin. All of us experience many of these sufferings as we pass through life. There is no immunity to them.

The most common of these sufferings are physical in nature. We have bruises, aches and pains. We suffer from disease, accident and catastrophe.

More serious are the sufferings that involve mental anguish. Such sufferings come to the unsaved and the saved alike. It is easy to point out such instances in all of our lives. Suffering is common to all mankind.

Another common anguish arises from seeing loved ones suffer. We, ourselves, do not have the pain, but we suffer as we see another become weaker and die. If we could bear the pain or even the death of that dear one, we would gladly suffer it within ourselves, but that is not possible. We suffer agony as we must watch all that life holds dear, from a human point of view, go on to death, while we are left to face the loneliness of life. But even such sorrow is tempered by the fact that we have life in Christ. The pain is not as great for the believer as it is for the unbeliever. Because we know the Lord is with us in the midst of our pain and suffering, it is easier to bear it.

SPIRITUAL SUFFERING

But there is another kind of suffering of whose existence the world is completely unaware. No unsaved person can imagine the various burdens which confront the true believer year after year as he advances in the Christian life. These are spiritual sufferings. The natural man—the man outside of Christ—does not have them and cannot receive them. He cannot receive the things of the Holy Spirit, for they are foolishness to him, neither can he know them, for they are spiritually discerned or known. (1 Cor. 2:14)

There is a realm of spiritual suffering that comes from

without because we are followers of Christ. Persecutions, lies, and accusations will arise from those outside the household of faith. But we are told:

"Blessed are they which are persecuted for righteousness' sake: for theirs is the kingdom of heaven. Blessed are ye, when men shall revile you, and persecute you, and shall say all manner of evil against you falsely, for my sake. Rejoice, and be exceeding glad: for great is your reward in heaven: for so persecuted they the prophets which were before you."

(Matt. 5:10–12)

But, the most grievous of all our sufferings, are those which take place WITHIN, in the sanctuary of the soul, and are known only to our Heavenly Father. We could enumerate these, but I want to emphasize here an entirely different kind of inner suffering, one which is a part of the Christian life. This suffering is called "a groaning." The Apostle Paul said it this way:

"For we know that the whole creation groaneth and travaileth IN PAIN together until now. And not only they, but ourselves also, which have the first fruits of the Spirit, even we ourselves GROAN WITHIN ourselves, waiting for the adoption, to wit, the redemption of our body."

(Rom. 8:22,23)

IN LABOR

Paul, speaking to the Romans and to us in very graphic language, is saying the material universe around us is groaning because it is in a childbearing time. Almost any student of history can see that the pains are becoming more intense and the contractions are coming at increasingly short intervals. We have only to count the years between modern wars to see that the whole world is in labor and the pains are becoming more intense.

The creation cannot rest until the plan of God is fulfilled and those who have been called in Christ come to the FULL BIRTH OF THE NEW LIFE which lies before them. Then they will have been manifested before the universe as the sons of God, and will have entered into all the fullness which will come to them at that moment.

The true Christian is not disturbed at the erosion of the fields, the tornadoes, the typhoons, the hurricanes, the earthquakes, and the other catastrophes of nature which frame our earthly existence. Or is the child of God disturbed at the wars, famines, pestilences, and other cataclysms which touch the human race. He knows all of them are according to the great eternal plan of an all-wise and all-loving Heavenly Father who is bringing to pass all the counsels of His own will.

Jesus said that in the days prior to His second coming, the creation would be groaning all around.

"And ye shall hear of wars and rumours of wars: see that ye be not troubled: for ALL these things MUST COME TO PASS, but the end is not yet. For nation shall rise against nation, and kingdom against kingdom: and there shall be famines and pestilences, and earthquakes, in divers places. ALL THESE ARE THE BEGINNING OF SORROW (pain)."

(Matt. 24:6–8)

The Bible makes it plain that the true child of God also will experience labor pains. Phillips' translation puts it this way:

> "It is plain to everyone with eyes to see that at the present time all created life groans in a sort of universal travail. And it is plain, too, that we who have a foretaste of the Spirit are in a state of painful tension, while we wait for that redemption of our bodies which will mean that at last we have realized our full sonship in him."
>
> (Rom. 8:22,23)

SPIRITUAL GROANINGS

We who have the Holy Spirit groan because our true sonship is not yet realized, that we are separated from the completeness of the purposes of God, and are not yet in the state for which we were created.

In the beginning of our Christian life, the groaning might be likened unto a faint moan in most of us. In my own life, through my teens and early twenties, I grew very slowly in God and was addicted to the things of the world for a number of years. Finally, I began to leave the baby stage and enter a new realm in God.

The Apostle Paul had much the same experience. He said:

> "When I was a child, I spake as a child, I under-stood as a child, I thought as a child: but WHEN I BECAME A MAN, I put away childish things."
>
> (I Cor. 13:11)

I wonder how many of you are yet children when it comes to spiritual things?

The groaning which characterizes the believer is a desire to BE FINISHED with the life of the world that we may enter into the reality of another—ETERNITY. WE WAIT FOR THE "REDEMPTION OF OUR BODIES."

This REDEMPTION OF OUR BODY is the final phase of our salvation. It is what Peter spoke about when he wrote:

> "Blessed be the God and Father of our Lord Jesus Christ, who according to his abundant mercy has begotten us again unto a lively (living) hope by the resurrection of Jesus Christ from the dead, TO AN INHERITANCE incorruptible, and undefiled, and that fadeth not away, reserved in heaven for you, who are kept by the power of God through faith unto salvation READY TO BE REVEALED IN THE LAST TIME."
>
> (I Pet. 1:3–5)

This is the salvation which our Lord Jesus Christ has provided for us. If you are born-again of the water and the Spirit, God has begun the work of salvation in you and He will finish it.

> "He that hath begun a good work IN YOU will perform it unto the day of Jesus Christ."
>
> (Phil. 1:6)

BODY REDEMPTION IS FUTURE

Let me repeat, the redemption of the body is the final phase of our salvation. The Bible teaches this will take place at the second coming of Jesus Christ, NOT before.

Some are so anxious to be glorified that they are teaching

you can enter into an immortal body and experience the "redemption of the body" now, while you live in this secular sin-infested society.

Other deceived individuals are baptizing unlearned and ignorant people into immorality. These people are deceivers. They are deceived, are being deceived, and are deceiving others. They cast an intolerable burden upon poor people. They teach them they will not die even if Christ should tarry for 100 years. And if they die, it is only because of their lack of faith. As the deceived ones become older and feebler, they despair of the grace of God. They discover they have a yoke about them which is impossible to bear.

THE LAST TRUMP

The Bible DOES NOT teach the redemption of the body prior to the second coming of Christ. It is plain from the Scriptures that the redemption of the body and the resurrection of the dead will transpire at the same time. Here are the clear words of Paul to the Corinthians:

> "Behold, I shew you a mystery; We shall not all sleep (die), but we shall all be changed, in a moment, in the twinkling of an eye, AT THE LAST TRUMP: for the trumpet shall sound, and the dead shall be raised incorruptible, and WE SHALL BE CHANGED."
>
> (I Cor. 15:51,52)

The resurrection change to both the living and the dead will take place at the last trump. The last trump is connected with the second coming of Christ in I Thess. 4:16.

"For the Lord himself shall descend from heaven with a shout, with the voice of the archangel, and with the TRUMP OF GOD: and the dead in Christ shall rise first: then we which are alive and remain shall be caught up together with them in the clouds, to meet the Lord in the air: and so shall we ever be with the Lord."

At the coming of Christ, if we are in our graves we will be raised from the dead, and if we are alive and remain we shall be caught up together with them in the clouds, to meet the Lord in the air: and so shall we ever be with the Lord.

At the coming of Christ, if we are in our graves we will be raised from the dead, and if we are alive we shall be changed. The whole creation is waiting for this redemption which is the resurrection of our bodies. The groaning of the animate and inanimate creation will continue until the day when we, who have been redeemed by the Lord Jesus Christ, shall come into the fullness of our salvation and receive our eternal bodies.

WHAT A DAY THAT WILL BE!

Though we love our families, our homes, our friends and the good things of this life, there is an inner groaning and suffering. The Christian knows he has been "born of God" for a reason—one not yet attained but which he longs to see.

" . . . but though our outward man perish, yet the inward man is renewed day by day. For our light affliction, which is but for a moment, worketh for us a far more exceeding and eternal weight of glory: while we look not at the things which are seen, but at the things which are not seen: for the things which are seen are temporal; but the things which are not seen are ETERNAL."

(2 Cor. 4:14–18)

KEEP YOUR EYES UPON ETERNAL THINGS!

If you have enjoyed this book, you will want to read other inexpensive publications published and distributed by WHITAKER BOOKS.

Over 300 other books and cassettes are available to accommodate your needs. Two of these books are advertised on the next page of this book. They are bestsellers. To order these or any of our publications, please mail the coupon below. Good quantity discounts will be shown in the catalog.

------------------------ DETACH HERE ------------------------

WHITAKER BOOKS
504 Laurel Drive
Monroeville, Penna. 15146
Phone: 412 372–6420

Please send me a free catalog on your publications:

Name_____

Address_____

_____ Zip Code_____

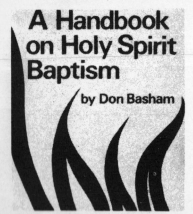